The Hospitality Mentality

Endorsements

"Unlike so many others, Josh makes clear the distinction between what's a service and what's an experience, showing you how to be both efficient and engaging, have high productivity and offer a great performance, and meet guest expectations while staging a wow experience. Analyze your business through the lens of *The Hospitality Mentality* and it will never be the same again."

—**B. Joseph Pine II**, coauthor, *The Experience Economy: Competing for Customer Time, Attention, and Money*

"In *The Hospitality Mentality*, Josh lays out a framework that is intuitive and actionable, and gives the reader the tools needed for every member of your team to "wow" every guest, every time, and create loyalty through the emotional impact of the experience."

—**Dan Cockerell**, Disney Keynote Speaker, Former Vice President of Magic Kingdom

"*The Hospitality Mentality* covers all aspects of the right mindset to make your guests feel appreciated in a way, that it will drive your business. Mixed with many real-life examples, Josh summarizes the basic understanding of what it takes to get to the new level in terms of guest satisfaction. This should be read by every hospitality employee and leader, who wants to improve guest satisfaction and be more successful by exceeding the expectations of each one of their visitors."

—**Jakob Wahl**, President and CEO, International Association of Amusement Parks and Attractions

THE Hospitality MENTALITY

---- 🍍 ----

Create Raving Fans Through Your Guest Experience

---- 🍍 ----

Josh Liebman

NEW YORK

LONDON • NASHVILLE • MELBOURNE • VANCOUVER

THE  MENTALITY

Create Raving Fans Through Your Guest Experience

Published in New York, New York, by Morgan James Publishing in partnership with Magic Press. Morgan James is a trademark of Morgan James, LLC. www.MorganJamesPublishing.com

Proudly distributed by Publishers Group West®

Morgan James BOGO™

A **FREE** ebook edition is available for you or a friend with the purchase of this print book.

CLEARLY SIGN YOUR NAME ABOVE

Instructions to claim your free ebook edition:
1. Visit MorganJamesBOGO.com
2. Sign your name CLEARLY in the space above
3. Complete the form and submit a photo of this entire page
4. You or your friend can download the ebook to your preferred device

ISBN 9781636981765 paperback
ISBN 9781636981772 ebook
Library of Congress Control Number: 2023934476

Cover and Interior Design by:
Chris Treccani
www.3dogcreative.net

Illustration & Interior Graphics by:
Abigail Giganan

Morgan James is a proud partner of Habitat for Humanity Peninsula and Greater Williamsburg. Partners in building since 2006.

Get involved today! Visit: www.morgan-james-publishing.com/giving-back

To my wife, Franny, who encouraged me throughout the entire journey of writing this book, and to our son, Jacob, who allows me to see the guest experience through the lens of a child

Table of Contents

Preface

During the colonial days of America, early settlers would leave their homes for weeks or months at a time to explore regions that they had yet to discover. Given the dangers of these expeditions, many wouldn't return unscathed, and many wouldn't return at all. Those that did, however, brought back stories of adventure, triumph, and friendship, along with souvenirs to share with their family and friends. The souvenirs would include exotic fruits and spices, all indigenous to the regions they explored. One of the most popular keepsakes was the pineapple.

Eventually, the explorers began posting a pineapple on a spear in front of their home to declare their return. This would spark curiosity and confusion, considering no one had seen anything like it before. The pineapple served as an announcement, as well as an invitation, for all to come and celebrate the return. Neighbors and townspeople became guests in an immersive storytelling environment that would fill them with wonder, as they learned about encounters with locals, encounters with animals, and the most incredible culture and foods that could ever be imagined. There was always plenty to share, including the now-famous pineapple.

For hundreds of years, the pineapple has been internationally recognized as the symbol of hospitality. The pineapple is a signal that welcomes strangers and friends alike, inviting them into a comfortable environment where they are made to feel at home, and it can create extraordinary experiences that make a meaningful impact on their lives. Nowadays, representations of a pineapple can be found at the entryway of buildings, in marketing material of hospitality organizations, and in other environments that send the message that all are welcome.

In a business setting, we can all strive to seek the core of the pineapple, also known as the Hospitality Mentality, and create a service culture that leads to personal, professional, and financial success.

Introduction

There is a common thread among the best hospitality operators throughout the world, including destination resorts, tourist attractions, family-owned and operated boutiques, or small leisure venues that holds them all together: the Hospitality Mentality. The deliberate desire to provide a superior experience is measured not only by the smiles on the faces of those experiencing it but also by creating the desire to repeat the experience, share the experience with as many people as they can, and preserve the memory for a lifetime. This mentality is one of the core components of success. Better yet, it can be measured, fine-tuned, and repeated as an operational practice.

The Hospitality Mentality is crucial to success, regardless of the industry you are in. We will explore examples that come from some of the top hospitality leaders in the world and discuss how they can be applied throughout all business types. We will talk about how it applies to gaining repeat business, generating referrals and positive word of mouth, and ultimately, breeding loyalty from those you serve. The Hospitality Mentality goes beyond providing great service and having friendly staff; the outcomes include more guests, higher revenue and average spend, and expanded profit margins. The Hospitality Mentality will turn a transient consumer into a raving fan. When delivered consistently, your loyal fans will naturally create more loyal fans.

All of the concepts that we will discuss in this book are concepts that have no plateau—they can always get better. If your service is stellar, your online reviews are superb, and your social media following is higher than your competitors, I ask this: *Now what?* What happens next? You have raised the bar for what people expect when they do business with you, so what will you do to keep raising it further? If you deliver an excellent experience during someone's first encounter and then provide a regular or "good" experience the next, your guest might consider that a failure. Failure, as you will see, is not the end of the world, but it is never your goal to give good service if they're used to great.

If you don't strive to continually refine the Hospitality Mentality, you become complacent. With complacency comes decline, and a declining business quickly becomes an obsolete business. You will never be perfect, but you can always be better than today. The Hospitality Mentality is designed to drive loyalty through the experience you provide, not just the products or services you sell, and not the price you charge for it. Instead, the Hospitality Mentality allows you to command a *higher* price, resulting in higher revenue and reduced costs in marketing and advertising, because your raving fans are *doing it for you*.

Those who have excelled at the Hospitality Mentality show commitment to each stage of the journey that comes with everyone who walks through your doors, buys from you, books an appointment, hires your firm, or any other means of doing business with you. The process is universal to business-to-business, business-to-consumer, for-profit, or nonprofit organizations. The journey consists of what happens in the prepurchase, duration, and postpurchase phases, and the first three sections of this book reflect the primary goal of each phase: Set the Expectation, Exceed the Expectation, and Put Fuel on the Fire. In each section, we will break down each of these goals into actionable chapters that will provide the steps you can follow to optimize each area of the guest experience.

While these recommendations and anecdotes provide ample material to weave into your existing service training, the goal of this book is to help you communicate why any of this even matters. The framework of the Hospitality Mentality enables employees to be in the right headspace before being presented with service techniques; otherwise, this book would be called *Hospitality Best Practices*, and it would be up to you to determine how it would resonate with your team. When the Hospitality Mentality is embraced from day one, all other elements of service fall into place much more naturally.

Here is what you can expect from each section of this book:

- **Part 1: Set the Expectation:** To get started, we will develop the framework for defining your service culture, discover the main drivers behind loyalty, understand what guests anticipate prior to their visit, and determine what it means to meet their expectations.
- **Part 2: Exceed the Expectation:** In this section, you will gain the inspiration to weave in creative enhancements to your service culture that go beyond what your guests expect, from personalizing the experience to keeping enthusiasm consistent to anticipating guests' needs to providing "wow" moments.
- **Part 3: Put Fuel on the Fire:** Beyond exceeding expectations, you will build upon your service culture by making improvements through guest feedback, turning around

negative situations, driving repeat visitation and word of mouth, rewarding loyalty, and understanding the importance of celebrating every guest.

Each section contains four chapters. At the end of Chapters 1–12, a single sentence, or strategy statement, will be provided to summarize the key message of the chapter. Take note of these statements because you'll be instructed to use them after you finish reading the book. (Yes, there is bonus content! Stay till the end.)

I hope you enjoy the lessons, key points, and entertaining anecdotes along the way. And with that, please **be my guest** as we navigate the Hospitality Mentality.

PART 1:

SET THE EXPECTATION

The Hospitality Mentality begins with level-setting the expectation internally within your organization to ensure that everyone is reaching the same goal. This process crosses all departments and all lines of leadership and frontline staff. Depending on the size of your business, your frontline operational staff members may not have direct contact with marketing, although marketing is generally responsible for setting the expectation that operations teams need to deliver, as well as exceed. If frontline operations staff members are unaware of the objectives of the marketing initiatives, it can quickly turn into an unintentional misalignment that results in the guest suffering. And if the guest suffers, they begin to feel misinformed, which leads to frustration, anger, negative feedback, and eventually becoming an adversary of the business. Part 1 aims to prevent that.

This section will cover the following:

- **Chapter 1: First, Get Rid of Your Customers—Creating a Service Culture:** understand how disconnecting the transactional element from your experience makes your guests feel more welcome

- **Chapter 2: The Secret to Driving Loyalty:** understand the purpose of managing the guest experience and why this is crucial to the business
- **Chapter 3: Your Guests Don't Need You:** identify specifically what guests anticipate prior to arrival, along with why they are visiting, in order to set a proper baseline expectation
- **Chapter 4: Don't Put the Cart Before the Horse:** recognize why exceeding a guest's expectation cannot be achieved before ensuring that it is first met, and how to manage the experience in the correct order

Chapter 1:
First, Get Rid of Your Customers—
Creating a Service Culture

🍍

There was a hot dog restaurant in South Florida I used to eat at on occasion, nearly every time I was in the area. What I liked about the restaurant was that the food was prepared with high-quality ingredients, and the ambiance was a lot of fun—it had this grungy, heavy metal vibe that was done very well. It was different, yet welcoming. The menu was creative with a lot of unique offerings that you wouldn't expect at a hot dog restaurant or at most casual dining locations. The prices were reasonable and the value for the offering, in my opinion, was pretty high. And most importantly, you could tell that every single staff member was a genuine, friendly, nice human being.

It may come as a surprise then that I couldn't stand this place. The first time I went I had such a horrible experience that I assumed it was a fluke. How could an experience be *so bad* when on the surface this restaurant seemed like it was the perfect business? Great food, great ambiance, and great people should be a winning combination. I even went back the next day to give the business the benefit of the doubt, expecting that I would get the "real" experience that I should have had the day before. Yet, to my disappointment, I made the same observations as my first visit. I went back a few more times over several months and ate a lot of hot dogs as I tried to pinpoint what was going wrong here.

What I eventually realized was that this restaurant was missing a necessary element that dragged it down considerably. As you might expect by now, that element was the service culture that makes up the Hospitality Mentality. Hiring nice employees is a starting point, but you cannot hire nice people and expect them to deliver an experience that meets the standard you expect from them and that your guests expect from your business. It requires an intentional desire to see that the guest's expectations are met and exceeded, which is more than showing up for work and "checking the box" to get the job done. It also includes having contingency plans in place for when the expectation is not exceeded, to get the guest's experience back on track to where it should be. They didn't have it.

This restaurant had no formal seating process, yet there was no indication that guests could seat themselves. On each visit, I waited until a server passed by, where I had to get their attention, and they scratched their heads and pointed to a table that may or may not have been available and clean. My order was incorrect on *every single visit*, with minimal acknowledgment of any error. One time when ordering crispy hand-cut fries, I was brought a bag of baked potato chips, and when I brought up the error, I was told that it was intentional—they were out of fries, so they brought me what they felt was the next best thing, and hoped I didn't notice. The bill usually required a thorough review and led to a distrust of what I was being charged for. Getting an order wrong isn't the end of the world, but not caring about it is when I start to raise an eyebrow.

Most people would stop visiting, but I became more and more intrigued with how a business could have so many missteps in service delivery without attempting to correct them. I continued to go any time I was in the area. One day, however, I arrived at the restaurant to find that it was no longer in business. I genuinely felt sad for the owners, operators, and great people who were working there, but it was a direct lesson that hospitality standards can make or break a business. While I never knew the business's financial situation, my front-end observations led to how guests were being treated when they came to dine, and that ultimately turned people off.

When looking to diagnose what went wrong at this particular restaurant, I determined that the service culture ended when they hired nice people and put them to work. There was a clear lack of training and direction on how the service should be delivered, from the broad concepts down to the granular details that might go unnoticed when done right, but that were absolutely noticed when done wrong. It was obvious that they weren't immersed in the philosophy, informed of the strategy, or trained on the tactics that would allow the Hospitality Mentality to thrive. A favorable experience at this restaurant could simply be defined as the absence of detractors—which represents a *playing not to lose* mentality. Instead, you want to *play to win*. Playing not to lose is when you only play defense; you focus your entire energy on making sure things don't go wrong so that you can meet the bare minimum. Playing to win is when incredible experiences happen on purpose. They are carefully crafted, yet they feel serendipitous to the recipient.

What could this hot dog restaurant have done differently? This book aims to help you prevent the fate that this well-intentioned restaurant suffered.

The first step of implementing the Hospitality Mentality into your organization is a mindset exercise. Before focusing on operational procedures and uncovering creative ways to use service to yield success, you must first identify the audience you are serving. The starting point in this process is giving them a name, and more importantly, an identity. This sets the stage for applying the Hospitality Mentality throughout all levels and departments of your business.

What Do You Call the People Who Do Business with You?

If the title of this chapter seemed perplexing, here's why. Throughout the crowded lands of destination theme parks, the lounge chairs at five-star resorts, the massage tables at the best spas, and in the dining rooms of Michelin-starred restaurants all over the world, you will be hard-pressed to find a single customer. They simply do not exist. Search their websites, social media pages, and even look in their employee training manuals. The word "customer" is banned.

The reason why the hospitality industry claims to have no customers is not due to lack of business; by all means, *the best* organizations intentionally have no customers because a *customer* indicates a transaction but not does suggest any form of relationship. It is purely goods and services delivered in exchange for money. I give you money, you give me the thing, and we're done here. The word "customer" fails to acknowledge the journey that this individual or group has taken, from making the decision to patronize the business to the experience itself to how it lives on long after the transactional component is complete.

Instead, you will often hear the word "guest" in place of the word "customer" due to it having a more hospitable appeal. Using the word "guest" presents an interaction similar to if you were inviting them into your home, rather than just a realm in which you conduct business. Let's say you have friends over for dinner. You prepare for a guest's arrival, including cleaning, cooking, and arranging the furniture, so that you can show off that you were looking forward to seeing them. Giving them food is the compulsory action you must take in order for it to be considered a functional success, but you probably want to show that their visit is about more than removing hunger. By treating your business environment the same way (whether it is a physical location, online presence, or a fully remote service), you take the first step toward the Hospitality Mentality.

Simon Nash is the Owner and General Manager of Ohana Towels, a company that serves hospitality providers with warm, moist towels to elevate the guest experience.[1] Beyond providing towels to businesses, Simon's view of hospitality very much is about treating your guests as if they were in your home. In a hotel, if a guest leaves their toothbrush or toothpaste at home, how does the staff respond and react to the request? If they say no, they aren't failing to meet any particular expectation unless they specifically state that they provide these amenities upon request. But the Hospitality Mentality would suggest that you would want your guest to have this item, and you would do everything you could to make it happen. "When they bring it to you 10 minutes later, you look at it and say, 'Wow. That's what someone would do for me if I was staying with them at their house.' That's the hospitality piece. It's what you expect when you're staying with family, and when it's an environment where they *aren't* family, you leave with the same feeling that they looked after you first. It's an emotional element."

In *The Experience Economy*, a book that defines the difference between commodities, goods, services, experiences, and even transformations, authors B. Joseph Pine II and James H. Gilmore reference that experiences, in particular, provide a new source of value, thus changing how businesses refer to those who consume the experience along with those who deliver it. The authors comment on how the terminology specifically impacts which aforementioned category the business falls into, using Disney as the prime example, stating, "Rather than create another amusement park, Disney created the world's first *theme* parks, which immerse guests (never 'customers' or 'clients') in rides that not only entertain but also involve them in an unfolding story. For every guest, cast members (never 'employees') stage a complete production of sights, sounds, tastes, aromas, and textures to create a unique experience."[2]

While Disney is a textbook example, it is not the only business and theme parks are not the only industry that provides an experience worthy of eliminating the use of the word "customer." The key element of this observation is when the user is so immersed in the experience that you provide and the manner in which you stage it, they should no longer feel that they are a transient customer, but instead, feel that they are part of it. The same goes for employees, who are not merely performing a function of a job but providing an encounter that should result in a bond between the one delivering the experience and the one consuming it, leaving a lasting impression of the personalized interaction and a favorable view of the business once the experience is complete.

The Hospitality Mentality Is Not about Customer Service. It Is about the Guest Experience.

I never say "customer service" anymore.
That's not a thing, at least not with me.
—Ruddy Harootian

Ruddy Harootian[3] runs an art-focused tour in New York City. "It's definitely 'guest experience.' The phrase 'customer service' builds a wall in my mind." Ruddy explains that his hospitality philosophy is about building a relationship that is often a two-way street, where he can learn from them and ultimately build rapport. By establishing commonalities that build rapport with your guests, you no longer feel as if you are simply serving them from a functional standpoint, but rather ensuring that their experience is a positive one because you genuinely care. The relationship extends beyond a service provider and the individual paying for it, and instead, it blooms into a meaningful connection, where the transaction is merely an element of the greater value.

Simon Nash also has thoughts on the difference between customer service and hospitality. "Customer service is a very rational piece. Black and white, there it is. You need something, you've got it. Hospitality, on the other hand, is how you do it, how you make them feel, and how you are looking after them as a person first. And you've got an emotional element involved that is difficult to describe. It's personal. It's special for each person. But ultimately, it provides them with a feeling that this place is really unique because they noticed me as a person. They noticed me not as a number. They cared for me, and wow, that was a great experience. And ultimately when you're choosing it the next time, you turn to them first."

Rather than thinking of the transaction, think about what they are doing and how they interact with your business that makes them feel a part of it. Airlines have passengers, taxis and rideshares have riders, and fitness centers have members. Cultural tourism facilities, such as museums, aquariums, and zoos, often use the word "visitor" in place of customers, which suggests the same hospitable approach as guests. If you are struggling to come up with what to name your customers, the word "guest," while synonymous with hospitality, is certainly not exclusive. Shoppers in a retail or hardware store can be guests, and so can riders on public transit. Target stores have replaced "customer" with "guest" to make them feel more welcome compared with when they visit other similar retailers. For business-to-business organizations, try switching out "clients" for "partners"—you will be seen as a partner back to them, instead of as a vendor or supplier.

Implementation of the word "guest," or whichever term best defines your users, is an intentional decision to weave into the company culture. It will not necessarily come naturally, especially if the word "customer" has been the norm. It will require the word "customer" to be replaced in all training materials, internal communications, and any policies and procedures. It also must be communicated to all lines of staff members across all departments with the message that you do not (or no longer) view your guests as customers, and the reasons as to why must be reinforced. Stressing the message that the word "customer" suggests a transaction, rather than a relationship, will support your reasons for making these shifts.

Whatever you determine to be the best-fitting term to replace customers and employees, make sure it reflects how they use your product and shows that they are more than just a purchase. For the same reasons, you want to avoid putting a square peg in a round hole. A new term for the sake of a new term may come across as inauthentic, inaccurate, or just plain clunky. If a hardware store started referring to everyone walking through the door as a builder, home improver, creator, or fixer, it would probably sound forced, or at the very least confusing. Most likely, they would quickly regress back to being customers in the eyes of both employees and well, customers. Therefore, when in doubt, referring to these individuals as guests will always demonstrate the hospitable nature of your approach, regardless of your business type or the industry you serve.

For the sake of simplicity (mixed in with personal habit), this book will use the word "guest" as the primary term, with the exception of a few relevant quotes that refer to customers.

Creating a Service Culture

If you, your coworkers and colleagues, and every level of staff consistently provide great service, then nothing happens by accident. Great service is more than a series of unrelated actions, but rather the byproduct of the culture that the organization embodies. With a strong focus on *consistency*, organizations that embrace the Hospitality Mentality know that they cannot deliver a great experience on occasion, during peak or off-peak times, or only when the best staff members are working—it must be felt in every interaction with every guest and every staff member . . . every time.

When your guest service culture is thriving, the guest experience is naturally elevated, as staff members are regularly delivering a superior experience without wondering whether they are doing the right thing or not. When the service culture is lacking, however, there is little or no desire for staff to go beyond guests' expectations, resolve guest complaints, or challenge their own levels of service that they can provide. A lacking service culture will quickly lose business to competitors, regardless of price or product quality. A poor experience with an otherwise adequate product is exactly that: a poor experience.

Without a focus on experience, what you provide becomes equated to a commodity. It can be duplicated anywhere by anyone else, and if their focus on experience is stronger than yours, it will be quickly recognized. Case in point? The chicken sandwich. Many restaurants, specifically fast casual and quick service chains can make a really good sandwich. But if you ask anyone in the United States to tell you who gives the greatest chicken sandwich *experience*, many people will quickly be able to tell you that the answer is Chick-fil-A. By focusing on a service-oriented culture that exceeds what one would normally expect when ordering fast food, Chick-fil-A ensures that a great chicken sandwich is just one of the best parts of its product. The experience that surrounds the food offering shows that the company realizes it isn't the only restaurant that can make a good chicken sandwich, and that the experience is what stops its product from being a commodity. Chick-fil-A embraces the Hospitality Mentality by creating a service-oriented culture that is ingrained in its hiring, ongoing training, and engagement.[4] It's the company's biggest differentiator and therefore acts as its competitive advantage.

Many service-oriented skills are learned, which means most people aren't born with the mindset of delivering a superior experience. *That's okay.* Through training, coaching, and encouragement, employees can gain the necessary attributes as they regularly sharpen their skills—which takes time, practice, and intention. Since most of this development happens on the job and often requires making a few mistakes along the way, your hiring practices should reflect that you are bringing in people who will grow into their role. That said, requiring candidates to have years of guest service experience will significantly limit your talent pool and will often result in hiring staff members who may be overqualified for their roles. Since entry-level guest-facing positions can often be someone's first job, they probably aren't showing up to their interview with an extensive résumé. Therefore, the "tell me about a time you dealt with a difficult guest situation" question might not apply to someone who has never been employed previously.

But they shouldn't be eliminated from the talent pool. The interview process needs to screen for their *intention* to deliver a superior experience because you are hiring them for their future, not for their past. In that case, questions should foreshadow how they will deliver your service standards and handle situations that are sure to come up.

Start with the Basics

If you treat your work environment like your home, and those you interact with as if they are visiting you specifically, you present yourself with the innate desire to serve. This does not necessarily mean that you are at their beck and call, obeying their orders and commands, but "to serve" suggests that you are genuinely interested in their satisfaction and their well-being during the time that they are within your domain. In order to do this, you must demonstrate the basics.

Perhaps the basics come naturally to you, or perhaps you've refined them over the years. When they are embedded into your operational culture, you move out of the mindset of the customer and into the mindset of the guest. You are no longer as concerned with the transaction as you are with the experience—and the experience is what will define the size of the transaction and how many more transactions there will be in the future. The basics of guest service must be put into action at all times in order to implement a guest-centric mentality, rather than a transactional experience. Take a look at the nine fundamentals of guest service, which act as the foundation for any positive guest experience. Whenever you are in front of guests, make sure you meet the following basics:

1. **Project a friendly attitude.** Always demonstrate a welcoming demeanor every moment that you are in front of guests. This can include walking to and from your work location and offering to assist guests who might appear confused or need help, regardless of whether you are on the clock or not. Never lose sight of the fact that your guests are visiting you with enthusiasm. A friendly attitude with a smile is a small gesture that goes a long way in showing guests that you're excited to be there too.

2. **Make eye contact.** Give your guests undivided attention by looking them in the eye when they approach, when speaking with them, and as you're sending them off. Not only is it respectful, but it also helps to build trust when guests have questions or concerns.

3. **Maintain proper posture.** Whenever possible, standing offers a more professional appearance in front of guests, and it creates a more welcoming environment. Your feet might hurt at the end of the day, so make sure to rest during breaks while you are back of house. In addition to standing, be sure to avoid slouching, being hunched over, or leaning against walls and countertops. Just like standing, proper posture gives off a much more professional appearance.

4. **Keep arms unfolded.** When your arms are folded, you are telling guests that you are reserved and unapproachable. It

might feel more comfortable, but with practice, you can eliminate the natural tendency to fold your arms.

5. **Keep hands out of pockets.** Try to recognize when your hands arc in your pockets—it might happen more often than you think. Instead, keep them at your sides, clasped together in front, or behind your back; whichever feels the most natural. Just like keeping your arms unfolded, keeping your hands out of your pockets shows guests that they can approach you.

6. **Greet the guest first.** Always strive to be the first to talk! Even if it is just a friendly "hello" or "good morning," greeting the guest first shows that you are there to help if they have a question. Better yet, pair this with making eye contact at ten feet and offering a verbal greeting at five feet for the best timing.

7. **Be in uniform.** Your uniform gives guests visual cues for who they can approach with a question or a concern. Being in full uniform (or a professionally dressed equivalent) while in front of guests shows that you are a professional and ready to help, especially when everything else on this list is also being met.

8. **Keep your phone away.** Get rid of all distractions! The guest in front of you is the most important, and especially when working in a safety position, a cell phone becomes a hazard unless it is completely out of sight. Check messages and social media on break and out of view of guests.

9. **No eating, drinking, or smoking.** Have you ever tried to ask someone for help while they were scarfing down a slice of pizza? Probably not, and if you have, then I'm guessing they weren't a big help. Keeping mealtimes confined to

breaks and never eating, drinking, or smoking in guest view shows that you can offer guests your undivided attention.

These guest service basics must be implemented by all staff members at all times while front of house and in guest view. This is the foundation for providing an excellent guest experience. While none of the basics are overly difficult to implement on their own, they do require a considerable amount of practice and learning to recognize when you are exhibiting the behaviors and when you are not. More importantly, leaders must constantly be on the lookout for staff members who may be slipping in one or more of the basics. This requires giving regular reminders and intervening as necessary to ensure that the basic standard is met. Because the basics can be broken as quickly as they are exhibited, they should always be top of mind because they will always be a concern. For instance, you will never eliminate leaning or slouching entirely, so plan to correct the course whenever observing staff breaking these basics while front of house.

Once you have mastered the basics, you can then focus on the next levels of guest experience: meeting expectations, exceeding expectations, and driving guest loyalty. But first, you must get out of the "customer" mindset and into the "guest" mindset. And a big part of that is saying "yes" whenever possible.

The Answer's Yes. What's the Question?

The Hospitality Mentality is a "yes" mentality, and a guest-centric mindset is a guest-*forward* mindset. It begins with a genuine desire to say yes and to accommodate guests' requests, regardless of how standard or how obscure they are. When the intention to accommodate is sincere, the guest experience thrives. This does not, however, suggest that you should meet every demand or say yes to everything, every time. It does not mean that the guest is always right when they are objectively wrong, but that your message to the guest is "I want to help you." The most fulfilling moments as a service provider can come from taking on an obscure request and seeing it through to a satisfactory finish.

Having a mindset that suggests that the answer is yes before hearing the question can lead to remarkable experiences that lead to exceeding expectations, whereas defaulting to declining out-of-the-ordinary requests can lead to unnecessary service failures. Take for example these two requests that guests made while staying in a hotel; one where the request was accommodated and the other where it was not. The first example comes from an article shared on ThePointsGuy.com about bizarre hotel requests:

> In 2015, Lauri Howe, director of communications for Boston's Seaport Hotel, shared one of the strangest requests her hotel had ever received. "The most memorable request for us is the guest who asked for 20 pounds of ice for his penguins," she told IndependentTraveler. com. "The penguins visited a year or two ago as part of one of the exhibits at the Boston Globe Travel Show. They stayed in the bathtub when they weren't on display at the show, which was held onsite in the Seaport World Trade Center. Twenty pounds of ice actually isn't too much, and we have multiple ice machines at Seaport, so we filled up four bags for them. We hope the ice helped to keep them comfortable during their stay!"[5]

It was an odd request, and one that would have been easy to say no to, but the Seaport took the opportunity to make it happen. Even though it was out of standard operations to fill up a bathtub with twenty pounds of ice for a penguin, the request was genuine, and the hotel acted out of a sincere desire to say yes, despite the unusual ask.

The second example happened to me. I was offered the opportunity to communicate with a hotel via text message instead of having to call guest services for standard requests . . . and my request was about as standard as they come, and no penguins were involved. Before packing for my trip, I realized at the last minute that I did not have any travel-size toothpaste and did not have time to run to the drugstore to pick up a tube. Fortunately, nearly every single hotel in the world is set up for this scenario and provides small amenities, such as toothpaste, shaving cream, or razors upon request. If you recall the example from Simon Nash from earlier in this chapter, I was hoping, and for what it's worth, expecting, that type of hospitable experience.

When contacting housekeeping via my guest room phone, I was placed on hold, and the recorded hold message asked whether I wanted to chat via text instead of waiting on the line. I inputted my phone number and the call disconnected, resulting in the following text conversation:

HOTEL: Thank you for choosing to text with me instead of staying on hold! How can I help? 😊

ME: Hi! Can you bring toothpaste to room 3106?

HOTEL: My apologies! We do not offer toothpaste via housekeeping. You are able to purchase that item at the [gift shop] located right by the guest elevators!

ME: I'm already back in my room. Can it be brought up to me and you can charge me for it?

HOTEL: Unfortunately, we would not be able to deliver items from the shop to the guest room.

Despite my frustration with the word "unfortunately" (more on this in chapter 10), I was first denied a simple and common request, and when I presented an alternative, I was denied again. My immediate thought was, *What is the point of having a text-based concierge if standard requests are going to be denied regardless?* If you are going to implement a tool or technology that helps your guests, the backbone of your operation must be one of accommodation. Technology itself does not make the Hospitality Mentality come to fruition; it must be a fundamental component of your service culture. And a big part of that culture is the desire to say "yes," whether it's for twenty pounds of ice to keep penguins chill, or to simply bring toothpaste to a guest's room. When the "yes" mentality is in place, making it actually happen becomes easier.

Now that we've covered the foundations of creating a service culture that results in the intentional desire for guests to have a positive experience, we can move to the next step of the Hospitality Mentality that shows us what happens when it goes right, and how it leads to guest loyalty. This all helps us set the stage for defining and meeting guests' expectations, leading us to deliver an excellent guest experience—*not* customer service.

Chapter 1 Strategy Statement:

We treat everyone who visits as a guest, rather than a customer, because they are more valuable than the transaction.

Chapter 2:
The Secret to Driving Loyalty

"Y ou coming tonight? This might be the best lasagna yet."

It's Thursday. Pam is asking every team member she can find whether they'll be coming over after work because she's hosting the entire crew. The ride is operating in the background as normal on a hot summer night. In between dinner invitations, Pam helps organize guests in the load station, telling certain guests that they should put their purse in a locker, secure their sunglasses, or make sure their baseball cap is tight enough— otherwise they might lose them on the ride. She questions the height of one small child, motioning to a ride operator and suggesting that they measure the child to make sure they meet the minimum height requirement. One guest complains about how long the line is, and Pam addresses it by assuring them that the team is doing all they can to move things along efficiently on a busy summer night. Then she goes back to building hype for this lasagna. Typical Thursday stuff.

It's probably worth mentioning at this point that Pam isn't paid to be there. In fact, she's *paying* to be there. She doesn't need to be doing any of this. Pam and her son, Ben, were active season pass-holders to Cedar Point who lived locally and visited the park multiple times a week. They were familiar faces to me, along with many other ride operators across the park. Everyone knew when Pam and Ben were there, yet she refused any VIP treatment. She visited like a normal guest, yet she was a secret vigilante who looked out for all of our best interests. It's one thing to buy season passes year over year, and it's another thing to use the pass so often that it maximizes its value. But it's on a whole new level to know as much about the operation as the staff do that you can do parts of their job, do it well, and enjoy being a part of it. Oh—and hosting the entire crew for lasagna multiple times each summer just to show her appreciation for their hard work? That's on another planet.

Now we ask ourselves, how can we get more guests like Pam?

If we are going to break down the individual components of the process, we must first identify what the long-term goal is, and ultimately, the destination of this road map. It's more than service, it's more than being nice, and yes, it's more than eliminating the word "customer" from your company's culture. The strategy that surrounds the Hospitality Mentality can be aligned with a single vision that will guide the individual components that make up the end goal—and they are outlined, in order, throughout this book. The vision can simply be summed up as ***achieving guest loyalty***. Guest loyalty is one of the most powerful drivers that move your business forward, as loyalty increases your volume of business, reduces marketing and administrative costs, increases brand awareness, and strengthens your reputation . . . all at the same time. By incorporating each element of the Hospitality Mentality throughout your organization, guest loyalty will be a natural byproduct.

Let us now look at what this really means. If I say, "loyal guest," what comes to mind? If we are going to dive into the nitty-gritty of how to achieve the Hospitality Mentality, it is important that we are clear on what we're talking about, particularly when it comes to guest loyalty. Loyalty is a concept that takes on many forms, but when looking to develop actionable steps, we need a definition.

Now that you have thought about what comes to mind, I am going to rephrase the question slightly. If I say, "loyal guest," not just *what*, but *who* comes to mind? Think about this for a second. Maybe you are thinking of a specific person who has met this qualification of loyal. Perhaps it's a family, parents, grandparents, or children, who you feel fall into the parameters of what it means to be a loyal guest. Do you have a Pam? Even if you can't think of a specific person, consider what that person would look like if they were a devoted fan of your business. They have proven their worth to you, and you acknowledge it by recognizing that they are loyal.

With that determined, what does that guest do to demonstrate their loyalty? The majority of this book will go through the process of breaking down how that guest became loyal, specifically the actions that *you* need to take to get there, but let's begin with the end in mind. We have reached loyalty with the guest (or guests) you are thinking about right now, or that you envision. What do they do on a regular basis, or at least with some frequency, that shows they are loyal? By understanding what actions loyal guests take, we can deconstruct the process and backtrack it to the point when they were first-time guests. They weren't born loyal to your business, so something must have happened between the point in their life when they were unaware of your existence to the point where they want to do business with you forever.

When it comes to what guests *do* when they've reached the status of genuine loyalty, we can look at three primary actions that guests take when they are loyal to your business. These actions are as follows:

1. **They return.** And not just once, they come back with some sort of average frequency. This doesn't necessarily need to be daily or weekly (although I have seen guests on a daily basis at multiple previous jobs—from my first job at a neighborhood frozen yogurt shop to several destination theme parks). They see your business as the only viable option that fills the void, even though you have plenty of competitors. They are on board with whatever you offer that enables multiple visits—whether it is an annual pass, season tickets, membership, or whatever encourages and rewards them to come back again and again. And not only do they have it, but they gain value from using it and truly getting their money's worth, and they plan to keep it going for the foreseeable future.

2. **They influence others to visit.** Your loyal guests are an extension of your marketing team. In many ways, they are actually *more powerful* than your marketing. Your loyal guests don't just come back by themselves, they bring their friends, family, neighbors, coworkers—whomever they can. If they're not accompanying them personally, then they are at least sending them to your door. And in today's online society, their audience is magnified exponentially through review sites and all other social media channels. They are actively working on your behalf, and they feel great when those whom they recommend are just as satisfied as they are with their experience.

3. **They stick up for you.** If influencing others to visit is playing offense, then you can bet that they will go to bat for you when the time comes. If someone they know had a bad experience while visiting you, they'll assure that person that their experience wasn't typical and that the poor

occurrence was surely a fluke. They're the experts on how to experience your offering to its fullest, and they may even help them avoid having a negative experience in the future. They also monitor your social media channels, and when someone tweets a nasty comment or makes a scathing post on your Facebook page, they will beat you to the punch by telling them that they were wrong and why. This benefit goes a long way because they will say the things that you never could. They are the best defense team you could ask for.

These aren't arbitrary factors; there is data to support these assertions with hard numbers. Loyal guests are five times more likely to purchase again and four times more likely to refer a friend to the company.[6] Loyalty isn't fluff. It is both a wellspring of revenue and a source of savings when it comes to guest acquisition and marketing. When you strive for loyalty with each and every guest, you find that loyalty breeds more loyalty, thus continually driving your revenue up and your marketing costs down. But remember, this goes in the other direction too, noting that your adversaries breed more adversaries, who replicate quicker and can damage your reputation faster than your loyal guests can strengthen it. This might sound discouraging, but this is all within your realm of control.

You might notice that among these three actions there were several that I did not mention. For example, "got the tenth punch on their card so their eleventh slice was free" does not suggest automatic loyalty. A punch card that rewards repeat visitation is exactly that—a repeat visitation program. Even those that are disguised as "loyalty programs" are mechanisms for you to complete only one of the three actions: returning to the business. Most would consider this to be loyal, and while that isn't entirely incorrect, once you've gained the reward, now what? They will stay on your program until they find another one that perhaps is similar. Even if your guests keep coming to earn the reward, this does not mean that they are going to influence others to visit, nor does it guarantee that they will defend you when needed.

When you master the Hospitality Mentality, loyalty programs only become vehicles for assisting your guests to achieve loyalty. Loyal guests do not need the punch card, whether physical, digital, or figurative. They are loyal to the product that you provide, the experience that you deliver, and the way in which you deliver it. Loyal guests connect with your mission, vision, purpose, and core values, and they seek it out because of a true desire. They may benefit from the tangible rewards that loyalty offers, and they absolutely should! They've earned it. However, if you want guests to genuinely connect with your business, this is achieved through their sense of the Hospitality Mentality. Reward programs are not the ultimate solution because you cannot manufacture loyalty.

So what's the secret to loyalty? Two words: guest experience.

Loyalty is a result of the guest experience. You cannot manufacture loyalty.

Don't get me wrong; I am not suggesting that repeat visitation programs are not effective. It would be hypocritical of me to suggest that, as I frequently enjoy the benefits that come with climbing the ladder on hotel chains' loyalty programs, annual passholder benefits at my favorite theme parks, access to comfortable airport lounges, and yes, even the wonderful taste of a free eleventh slice of pizza. However, if I were to narrow down the top businesses I frequent, any repeat visitation incentive would be an ancillary perk, and otherwise irrelevant. These types of programs have their place in influencing guests to return and can be highly effective as the push that guests need in order to commence their loyalty with you. They are the guest experience equivalent of training wheels. Repeat visitation incentives are like guest loyalty on beginner mode.

Why Loyalty Is So Important to the Health of Your Business

Before breaking down the methods of achieving the Hospitality Mentality and attaining guest loyalty, we must go over why this is important. The Hospitality Mentality is not a "soft" benefit to your business. Even in part 2, which will discuss methods for going above and beyond and providing great guest service, everything discussed in this book is geared toward improving attendance or visitation, increasing revenue through more purchases and *larger* purchases, and increasing overall profitability. One of the biggest challenges is implementing practices with every guest, every time, and with consistent buy-in from your colleagues, leadership, and frontline staff. If anyone suggests that the Hospitality Mentality is like a vitamin, which is "nice to have" every once in a while, you'll see primarily transient visitors and you'll continually have to churn out marketing campaigns to gain new business. Instead, initiatives geared toward hospitality and loyalty are life-sustaining nutrients—you *need* them in order to survive, thrive, and generate organic growth. Acquiring a returning visitor is substantially more cost-effective than generating new business.

Many consider guest loyalty to be the bridge between your company's marketing and operations teams. The goal of marketing is to bring guests to you, whereas operations teams control what you do with them once they're there. Guest loyalty is a result of what happens while they're on-site and how you use loyalty to fuel future growth and success. As mentioned previously, your loyal guests are an extension of your marketing team, thanks to the effectiveness of your operation, which can also be viewed as the guest experience. Today's best marketers are looking to loyal guests to act as influencers and help the marketers achieve their goals of promoting the brand, amplifying positive content, and driving traffic into your business.

Let's go back to your loyal guest (or guests) who came to mind at the beginning of this chapter. Do they still qualify and meet the definition outlined so far? Hopefully, to a degree, they have met at least one of the three primary actions—returning frequently, influencing others, and coming to your defense. Now, I want you to think about what *the most* loyal guest could look like. If there were a ceiling, where would it be? What are some specific actions that would suggest the pinnacle of guest loyalty for your business? Feel free to let your creative juices flow and disregard the parameters of being realistic. Even if what you envision might seem nearly impossible, getting halfway to an ambitious benchmark will still be substantially more impactful—and profitable—than setting the bar low. This type of thinking will also come in handy in chapter 8 when we discuss looking to create "wow" moments for your guests.

You will want to come up with specific loyalty actions for your own business and experience you offer, but here are some examples to get the ball rolling:

- They have access to visit your facility any time they choose (annual pass, membership, or subscription—any way that they have access on-demand and on their schedule).

- They use the above access so frequently that the card itself, if applicable, occupies prominent real estate in their wallet, alongside their identification and credit cards.
- They have left detailed, glowing reviews on every review site on which you are featured (Tripadvisor, Yelp, Google Reviews, Facebook Reviews, and any others).
- They follow every one of your social media accounts and regularly share your content with their network.
- When they visit, they share their own content online, tagging your business in their posts, and all posts are positive.
- When they visit, if something is inconsistent with your standard, they are quick to point it out in a constructive, optimistic, meaningful way, and through private channels (in person, email, phone—NOT through social media or review sites).
- In addition to sharing your content on social media, they read the replies to check for any adversaries, and they reply to them in a respectful but direct way that "sets the record straight."
- If you were to ask anyone in their social circle who they believe this person's favorite business is in your category, everyone they know will point in your direction.

If you have trouble coming up with ideas, think about businesses you are loyal to. What businesses are you promoting? Who would you go to bat for? Where do you send people if they ask for recommendations? Feel free to break outside your industry for this. This could be your cell phone service provider, restaurants, preferred kitchen appliances, an online course for parenting a newborn, or a brand of luggage. Who are you loyal to, and why? Now, think about what more your guests can do to exercise their loyalty to you. What is *your business* doing to weave *your way* into the fabric of *your guests' lives?*

Now, let's circle back to how we define guest loyalty. Using the three primary drivers, combined with the specific actions guests will take, here is our overarching definition of what constitutes loyalty:

> **Guest loyalty is a powerful force that occurs when the experience you provide has become an essential component of your guests' lives. Loyal guests will routinely visit your business, influence others to visit, and actively work toward ensuring that others are promoters of your business as well.**

Pam met the definition of a loyal guest.

If loyal guests are doing business with you on some sort of regular frequency and promoting your business to the outside world, they are your *promoters*. You want as many promoters as possible! However, let's consider the opposite type of guest, your *detractors*. Your detractors had a negative experience that was never resolved, and not only have they decided that they're not going to come back, but they have now taken it upon themselves to see to it that you do not succeed. They share negative word of mouth with their internal network of friends and family, and they post negative reviews on one or more review sites, with detailed narratives of their poor experience. They do the exact opposite of what your loyal guests do, and their effects can be more harmful than your promoters are helpful. Studies have shown that, on average, a dissatisfied guest will tell nine to fifteen people, and occasionally more than twenty, about a negative experience compared to a positive one.[7] The likelihood of these individuals converting into first-time guests after hearing or reading scathing reviews is minimal.

A negative experience can have serious consequences on your business when it comes to word of mouth. A negative review online will likely dissuade thirty potential guests[8] who were about to visit you, who have now changed their minds. Take thirty and multiply it by your average per capita spend, then by the average number of visitors per party, and then times twelve. If you get just one negative review every month, that is how much revenue you have lost over the course of a year. If your average spend is $50 with an average party size of three guests, then one negative review per month costs you $54,000 a year! That means that your detractors can cause a lot more damage than your promoters can influence!

However, guests having a poor experience is part of what we do. Of course, it is not what we set out to do, and you should never intentionally inconvenience your guests, but it certainly can be a part of many guests' experience with your business. Because of this, the steps toward achieving guest loyalty include identifying where many guests might be dissatisfied and taking quick actions to course correct. A service failure is not the end of the world, and in fact, it can be turned into a phenomenal experience for your guests that can quickly lead back to loyalty. You aren't going to knock it out of the park every time, nor should you expect that you will. If your business serves hundreds, thousands, or tens of thousands of guests on a daily basis, it is much more effective to build service recovery best practices for your team to follow, than to demand perfection from your staff. It just won't happen. If you believe that you can run a perfect operation and generate zero complaints, you are living in a fantasy world that doesn't exist. Or, if you do happen to run a business that receives no complaints, your communication channels are broken.

If your ultimate goal is to boost the financial health of your business, prioritizing guest loyalty will be your fastest route. Guest loyalty is achieved through delivering a superior guest experience, which is achieved when you exceed expectations. Exceeding expectations is an intentional act that occurs with every interaction that your guest has with your business. It requires meeting the baseline expectation that is defined by the promises that you made to your guests, which is what encouraged them to visit you to begin with. Many refer to this process as the guest journey, and the destination of this journey is loyalty. Your guests' journey might look something like this:

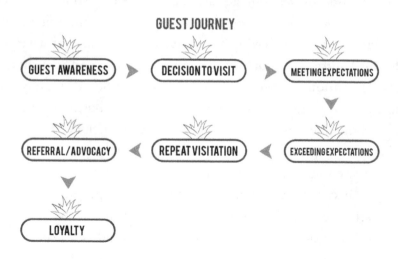

GUEST JOURNEY

GUEST AWARENESS ▶ DECISION TO VISIT ▶ MEETING EXPECTATIONS ▼

REFERRAL/ADVOCACY ◀ REPEAT VISITATION ◀ EXCEEDING EXPECTATIONS

LOYALTY

The above figure describes the guest journey as a linear experience that begins with awareness and ends with loyalty. However, when we layer in the benefits of guest loyalty, we can take this to the next level. Instead of the guest journey, I call it the *guest experience cycle* so that it implies that after their first experience, they begin planning their next, as repeat visitation is one of the most important factors of loyalty. The cycle begins prior to their visit, mostly occurs during their visit, and continues beyond their visit.

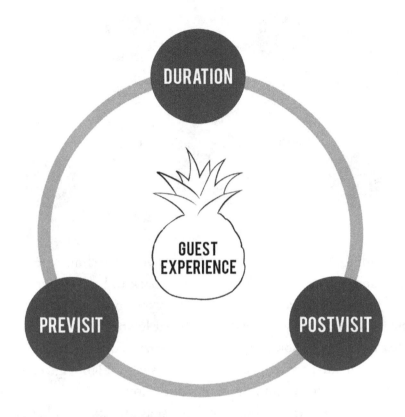

GUEST EXPERIENCE CYCLE

But wait! When done correctly, the guest experience cycle should not only start over but begin a new cycle for someone else, mimicking something closer to a figure-eight visual. The postvisit of one guest's experience should seamlessly lead to the previsit of another . . . and another . . . and another.

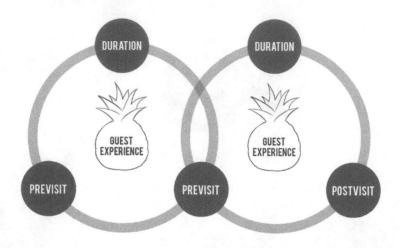

Think about the guest you chose as your benchmark for loyalty, and let's go back in time. Let's go back to before your guest was loyal, before they were satisfied with your business, and before they even visited for the first time. What happened along the way that took this person from having never visited you ever to committing themselves to your business to such a high degree? Let's start at the very beginning of the guest journey, in the previsit portion of the cycle, and start with guest awareness and what happened in the steps after the guest became aware of your business—before they became loyal.

At some point, something went right, and that guest's expectations were exceeded. By identifying what most likely went well for that guest, you can take these concepts and duplicate them by implementing them into your standard operations. The more guests whose expectations you exceed, the more loyal guests you are likely to gain. By methodically looking at what happens before a guest visits, what happens while they are visiting, and what happens afterward, you can take better control of the guest experience and turn your operation into a machine that produces genuine, organic guest loyalty.

So what's the secret to driving guest loyalty?

Guest loyalty is when guests come back often, refer others to visit, and come to your defense when necessary. Guest loyalty is achieved when expectations are exceeded on a regular basis.

Now it's time to work backward. To achieve guest loyalty, you *must* focus on exceeding your guests' expectations on a regular basis. If you are going to exceed expectations, you must first identify the best ways to *meet* these expectations. And before that, the overall guest expectation must be well-defined to ensure that you know what the target is that needs to be met and exceeded. In order to determine what that expectation is, you must ask a series of questions. These questions will be identified in the next chapter.

Chapter 2 Strategy Statement:

We acknowledge that true loyalty is a result of the guest experience, not loyalty programs, and therefore is driven by the service that we provide.

Chapter 3:
Your Guests Don't Need You

As we seek to understand your guests' expectations, we need to pull back and look at the guest experience from a broad perspective and slowly zoom in, like a plane flying at thirty thousand feet that slowly descends for a smooth landing. Beginning with the high-level overview, or the thirty thousand foot view, you will identify broad statements that suggest what it's like for someone to visit you. As your figurative plane lands, the picture becomes clearer and clearer as you begin to realize *why* someone would come visit you to begin with. To get to the landing, let's look at the following series of questions for you to consider when understanding what guests might anticipate that leads to their decision to give you their time, money, and attention.

What Do Your Guests Expect?
(Thirty thousand feet)

At thirty thousand feet, we are talking very general terms here. When you are at work every day, you are deep into the micro viewpoint of your business and looking at whatever is directly in front of you. What if you were to pull back for a moment and simply ask, "What do people expect when they give us their business?" What do they think is going to happen? At a very high level, we can come up with vague answers, but these answers might indicate your highest priorities. You may have multiple answers that either correlate or don't relate at all to each other, or you may have a singular definition of what guests expect.

In the leisure, tourism, and attractions industries, I'll frequently hear answers along the lines of "They expect to have a good time," "They expect to be treated with respect," or "They expect a clean facility." Guests at an amusement or theme park expect rides, at a zoo or aquarium they expect land and aquatic animals, coffee at a coffee shop, a room for the night at a hotel, and so on. The expectation, on the surface, is ultimately the core product that you provide.

Are Your Guests Visiting Out of a Need or a Want?
(Twenty-five thousand feet)

Even though the answer is obvious, it's not something that's always on our minds, and it's not on the minds of the staff who are seeing and doing this every day. Think of this scenario: here is a family that is excited to visit. They've set their alarms to wake up early, and they wake up before it even goes off because *today is the day*. They jump out of bed, have a quick breakfast, and then hop in the car for the single purpose of coming to visit *you*. The kids have their faces and hands pressed against the window in the backseat, and they barely even blink as they realize they're getting closer. They park the car, and they all jump out with excitement. They've made it. They're here.

I don't intend to put a square peg in a round hole here, so feel free to alter this part of the story so it properly fits the parameters of your business. Once that's set, hit pause, rewind, and now let's jump into a parallel universe that starts at the same moment that this story began. Your alarm goes off, and you hit snooze several times. It was a late night at work the night before. You stumble out of bed and do your best to wipe the sleep from your eyes. It looks like you slept in your uniform (maybe you *did* sleep in your uniform). No time for breakfast or caffeine; hopefully you can take an early lunch. You get in the car, fight traffic on your way to work, and pull into the parking lot. You get out of the car, you realize your shirt is untucked, and you quickly try to get yourself together before walking in.

The "you" in this part of the story can actually be you, your employees, your coworkers, or your boss. Regardless, these two worlds are about to collide. The moment of truth is about to come up that will determine whether that guest's expectation was exceeded, or whether it has fallen considerably below. And we know that this is not an everyday case for every staff member. On some days, perhaps everyone is jumping out of bed and just as excited to come to work as guests are to visit. It's unrealistic, though, to assume that every day is like that. After all, this *is* work, and it's often not easy work, and the stresses of any other job are still present—having to wake up in time, get ready to go, and manage constant pressing demands throughout the day.

When these two parallel universes meet, what will happen? That's why I ask you to think about whether your guests are visiting because they need to or because they want to. Even though the answer is obvious, how often do you think about it? When a guest approaches you or vice versa, I encourage you to think about not just the question, but about the answer. These guests do not have to be here. They made an intentional decision to visit and determined that this was going to be the most ideal option for them to spend their hard-earned money and their time. Whatever they are doing, they are likely doing so because they *want* to. Your guests don't need to visit you.

What Else Can Your Guests Do Besides Visit You?
(Twenty thousand feet)

This is another question that might seem obvious at first, but as we dive deeper into it, this is more than a simple competitive analysis. There are multiple layers to this question, each with an increasing amount of alternative options. You must consider all of the alternative options they have aside from visiting you:

Direct competitors. This is pretty straightforward. Your direct competitors are other businesses in your geographic region that provide a similar experience. Hotels compete with other hotels or alternative lodging options such as Airbnb and Vrbo. Restaurants compete with other restaurants nearby. Trampoline parks compete with other nearby trampoline parks. If you are the only business of your type in your local market, you may claim that you have no direct competitors, but that doesn't eliminate the notion of competition.

Indirect competitors. Pulling back a little, you acknowledge that there are other similar types of businesses that compete for the same demographic, chasing after their dollar and their time. If your business is categorized as "tourism," then anything else that falls into that space that is not the same type of attraction or destination as your business is considered an indirect competitor. A sightseeing cruise and an art museum provide very different experiences, but by serving the same demographic (guests visiting that region from out of town), they compete because you can only do one at a time. A family entertainment center competes indirectly with a movie theater, a wax museum competes indirectly with an observation deck, and a ski hill competes with a spa.

Everything else. Now we are stretching further out there. You have direct competitors and indirect competitors, so now what? Now there is everything else. Who does *not* operate in your space, but still occupies either money, time, attention, or all three, from individuals who would otherwise be your guest? If I choose to sit at home and binge-watch Netflix instead of leaving the house, then the streamers win. The hardest part is that the possibilities are endless.

By now, we have uncovered a couple of difficult truths. The first is that your guests don't need to visit, and the second is that instead of coming to visit you, your guests could literally do *anything else in the world*. In terms of trying to do business, the cards are not stacked in your favor. Realizing this, it's a miracle that anyone ever comes to visit you. There is no functional need for the guest to visit in order to survive, and the alternative options are limitless. The answers to the previous two questions suggest that every guest should be genuinely celebrated simply for having considered you! You need them far more than they need you. And if that's the case, the concept of guest loyalty is truly mind-boggling—if it is such an uphill battle to get someone in the door for a single visit, how can it even be possible that they would ever visit again, let alone actively work on your behalf to influence more business?

If your guests don't need you, and if they can be doing anything else besides visiting you, that leads to the next question as our plane continues to descend and get closer to the runway:

Why Do They Want to Visit?
(Fifteen thousand feet)
They don't need to visit you. They can do anything else besides visiting you, including visiting your direct competitors, visiting your indirect competitors, or occupying their time with any other activity—including functions that are actually needed (school, work, errands, home improvement projects, etc.). Therefore, the last question that remains to be answered is *why* your guests *want* to visit you.

Let's circle back to the first question asked in this trail—what do your guests expect? With our plane about to land, we need to quickly be reminded of what we saw from thirty thousand feet. The reason your guests want to visit is due to the expectation they have. For starters, this is partly due to the expectation that you set for them through your internal marketing but also based on what they've gained from other sources—previous experience, direct word of mouth from a personal connection, social media posts from those who are in or out of their network, and review sites.

After filtering through any or all of that, they have determined that they want to visit you because their expectation is *so high* that it exceeds all alternative options, including direct competitors, indirect competitors, and everything else (including doing nothing—inaction is also an option). Let that sink in for a moment. Your guests had endless possibilities on how to occupy their time and spend their hard-earned cash. This speaks volumes about what your guests expect their experience is going to be. And there is no reason for it to be any lower. Your goal, from a marketing standpoint, is to have an expectation that is so high that your business wins the *destination selection process*. This process might be conscious or subconscious or may fall anywhere on this spectrum. On the hyperconscious end, the guest is actively determining whether your business will be the right one. Imagine if they made spreadsheets and assigned weighted decision factors, like distance from home, price per person, and anticipated length of time, and ranked each of those in order of importance. The ultimate outcome is based on an objective decision that may or may not be combined with their gut feel. Most people probably don't do this, at least not nearly as involved, with the exception perhaps of major purchases—but the most thorough decision makers at least have this process running in their minds.

The flip side of the spectrum is the guest that might have stumbled onto your property on a whim, perhaps as an impulsive decision. There may have been less forethought and planning that went into it, and perhaps their expectation was not as high as they had not been served as much information as the guest in the previous scenario. They might be easier to please, but the same two factors still apply: the guest didn't need to visit, and they could have done anything else instead. Therefore, regardless of the forethought and planning that went into their visit, you are still tasked with focusing on exceeding their expectations in order to have a shot at generating loyalty.

Following the preceding list of questions is one question that stands out: *what happens when a guest does business with you?*

What's the Transactional Exchange?
(Ten thousand feet)

Now that we have brought a few details into focus through the previous four questions as our plane descended, we have determined that your guests visit you out of a genuine desire, and it is due to the high expectation that they have. However, we still have not specifically uncovered what it actually is that they expect. To answer this, let's define what they are receiving in exchange for giving you money. Set your business aside for a moment and take a look at businesses with which we all have some degree of familiarity. What is the transactional exchange at the following businesses?

- Starbucks
- Whole Foods
- Chevron

If you answered coffee, groceries, and fuel, respectively, you probably have realized that the question was quite straightforward. When I go to Starbucks and give them money, they give me coffee. When I go to Whole Foods and give them money, I walk out with groceries. When I go to Chevron, I give them money, and in exchange, I drive away with a full tank of gas that I did not have previously. These are all easy answers because they are all products that are relatively straightforward. When I come to visit an experience-based business, I pay money and I get . . .

A receipt? A room key? A directional gesture? A ticket? A flimsy piece of paper? Maybe a wristband? An email? A stamp on the back of my hand? While the specific answer will vary depending on your business and how you fulfill these types of transactions, we all know quite well that these are all incorrect answers. These items are purely the vehicle for what's about to happen. The actual takeaway that makes up the transactional exchange, or the deliverable that you provide when your guests come in and give you money, is an ***experience*** that creates a ***memory***.

There is a common link between a cup of coffee from Starbucks, a bag of groceries from Whole Foods, and a tank of gas from Chevron. These are all real things. Each of these is a tangible good that has substance and form. We know when it's there, and we know when it's not there. We have a full sense of awareness of each of these items, and we can take them with us when we leave the location where we bought them. You can't say the same about the deliverable of hospitality, which is an experience and a memory. These intangible concepts are consumed upon delivery; therefore, the instant that a guest leaves, they no longer have what you've sold them. It's been fully devoured. Additionally, the three items presented as an example can all be replenished and restocked when they're low on supply or gone (hence that little indicator light that comes on in your car when you're running low on fuel). Not hospitality.

The memory of an intangible experience lasts longer than tangible stuff, even though the experience itself might be over. Colin Shaw, Founder & CEO of Beyond Philosophy, LLC, and cohost of *The Intuitive Customer* podcast, put it quite nicely: "People don't choose between experiences. They choose between the memory of an experience."[9] This is not usually what is going through the minds of your prospective guests or even your own mind when considering an experience, whether it is a destination vacation or going out to dinner. At the surface level, you are selecting the experience that you anticipate you will enjoy most while you are in it. Deeper down though, as Shaw suggests, you will select the experience that you enjoyed the most when you recount the moments after it has been completed. We don't want to do the thing as much as we want to have done it.

As a quick aside, it would be imprudent not to recognize the value of the tangible component of tourism and hospitality. Souvenirs, including apparel, plush toys, and high-quality photography, are all tangible products, and they create a physical representation of the experience, which enhances the memory. Your guests purchase these items because it is as close as possible to leaving with the experience. However, most guests do not visit with the sole purpose of browsing the gift shop; they visit the gift shop because of the experience they had. Kenny Funk, who oversaw retail operations at Walt Disney World and then later at Great Wolf Resorts, says that retail is the gratuity that a guest leaves after their visit. "Guests will want to commemorate their amazing experience with a tangible reminder,"[10] meaning that if they enjoyed their experience, they buy a souvenir to show their appreciation for it. Revenue from retail is a reflection of a positive experience, and the souvenir that they take home prompts them of the memory that is intangible.

When comparing your business model to that of coffee, groceries, and fuel, you cannot apply the same logic to an intangible concept like an experience or a memory. A guest will not say, "I no longer have the memory of my experience, so I need a new one." In fact, the opposite is true. Your guests should have the desire to return *because* the memory they were provided with and the experience they had were so powerful that they need to experience more. The experience is what drives the memory, and the memory is what should drive new experiences.

So what do your guests expect? They expect that you will provide ***an experience that leaves them with a lasting memory***. But we can't stop there.

Breaking Down the Expectation
(Five thousand feet)

If this chapter ended right now, and the single takeaway was that your guests expect you to provide an experience that provides a memory, there would still be some degree of ambiguity. There is certainly more clarity now than the thirty thousand foot view that asks about what guests expect in broad terms, but we can unpack these concepts even further. We need to identify the building blocks of what makes up the experience and a memory, and even though they are somewhat subjective and nondefinitive, this will still be an excellent starting point for understanding the baseline of what guests expect. We can break this up into smaller chunks that define the concepts and categories that are a part of your operation, all of which are factored into guests' expectations. As we look even closer, we know that your guests expect you to be some form of the following:

SAFE OPEN EFFICIENT CLEAN

WELL MAINTAINED ENJOYABLE FRIENDLY AN ESCAPE

Safe. Safety is indisputably the highest priority of the guest experience. When people walk into a space that is not their own, whether they are traveling, in some sort of leisure mindset, or even completing routine out-of-home tasks throughout their day, are they always thinking about their safety? Hopefully, they are to some degree, but ultimately your guests expect (and even assume) that you have their safety in your best interests. Therefore, rules are present and properly enforced, heavy machinery is inaccessible to the general public, all hazards are prominently posted, and so on. Your guests expect to be safe when visiting your venue, and they expect you to look out for them.

Open. It seems obvious, but if your operating hours indicate that you open at 10:00 a.m., but you don't open until 10:45 a.m., then this is an expectation that has not been met. I once visited an amusement park that opened on time—as expected—and when I went to the ride that I wanted to ride first, the attendant at the entrance told arriving guests that they had just realized when they filled out their opening checklist right before opening that they didn't have a fire extinguisher, and that their supervisor was trying to find one. This delayed the ride's opening, failing all guests of what was otherwise a simple expectation. While it was necessary and showed that safety was their higher priority, it resulted in an inconvenience, and therefore a service failure, for all guests who expected the attraction to be open at the promised time. Except for extreme circumstances, your guests expect that you will be fully operational when you say you will.

Efficient. Your guests expect that you will be properly staffed for the anticipated business of season, day, or hour. They expect that lines will move smoothly, registers will be open, and that bottlenecks will be kept to a minimum. While your guests don't know the granular details of your operation such as throughput expectations or queue capacity, they can still identify if operations are moving slower or on pace with what they should be. When efficiency is lacking, their expectations are not being met.

Clean. Your guests may be forgiving of small pieces of trash or clutter here and there, but ultimately they expect that the cleanliness standard will be kept high. They expect that your floors, grounds, and pathways will be primarily clean and free of trash and debris, countertops will be wiped off and free of dust, retail shelves will be properly stocked and organized, and food service areas will be immaculate at all times. They want to enjoy an environment where they know that all staff members in all departments are committed to ensuring a high standard of cleanliness at all times.

Well maintained. Just like cleanliness, your guests expect that there is a strong commitment to keeping a facility that is free of wear and tear, freshly painted when needed, and fully functional at all times. This includes your heavy machinery and large fixtures down to door hinges and light bulbs. The cleanliness and maintenance of your operation make up the environment through which the experience is delivered to your guests, and there will be significant impacts if they are not continuously tended. Take a look at any review site and you'll see that just like cleanliness, maintenance is a top category in reviews of location based experiences—both good and bad observations are posted frequently.

Enjoyable. If you have won the destination selection process, outshining all competitors and alternative options, then your guests expect that the experience of visiting you will be more pleasant than standing in line at the DMV to renew their driver's license (no offense the any DMV employees reading this, but the reputation isn't the greatest!). They expect to be immersed in the environment that you've created, and they expect that their decision to visit you will be reinforced through having an enjoyable experience. If they did not expect to enjoy their time with you, they would have chosen something else.

Friendly. This wouldn't be the Hospitality Mentality if I did not mention friendliness! If guests are visiting you out of a want, rather than a need, then they expect that the staff with whom they will be interacting are also there because they want to be, not just because they need to be. They expect to be greeted quickly and pleasantly, with a smile and an-upbeat attitude. They expect name tags to be worn (if applicable) and uniforms to be wrinkle-free and worn appropriately. They expect the staff will also acknowledge in some way that guests are visiting out of a desire, rather than necessity, and act as such. They expect that the staff will have guests' best interests in mind. But remember, friendliness is not the definitive driver of the Hospitality Mentality. Great service is about more than being nice. It's critical, but this would be a short book if that were the case.

An escape. Lastly, the intangible product that we deliver is an opportunity for the guest to place aside the struggles that are common to everyday life. You are telling them that they can step out of the "daily grind" of work, school, and other responsibilities and truly take the time off. You provide a space that is free of bosses and the chores, errands, and obligations that they are used to performing as part of their regular routine. To be clear, you don't have to be a major theme park or a destination resort to be an escape. If you provide an hour's worth of enjoyment or entertainment that puts a smile on people's faces, you are a purveyor of escapism. You are the charging station for the batteries in our system that we are wearing down to their core. You are the cure for cabin fever. Your guests expect some degree of escapism.

By no means do I claim that this list is fully comprehensive of what your guests expect when visiting you. Depending on the nature of your business, it is likely that you can add to this list. A cultural attraction, including zoos, museums, and aquariums can add **Educational** and **Inspirational** to the list of what guests expect, whereas an amusement park might add **Thrilling**. The purpose of listing out each of these items is to identify the general baseline of how to define your guests' expectations. If you were to add all of these together, put them in a blender, and puree them, you would turn it into *an experience that leaves them with a lasting memory*. And that expectation is greater than the expectation of any alternative—whether it is your direct competitor, indirect competitor, or anything else, because your guests don't need you.

We have successfully landed at our destination.

I encourage you to continue adding to this list to include components that apply specifically to your operation, and indicate what they truly mean from the guest's perspective. Then, it must be recognized that this is the framework that dictates how the facility is operated. Each component in this list can be elaborated significantly, with multiple standards and procedures applied to each one. By carefully considering each component both individually and as part of the whole, you have a clear vision that will allow you to meet and then exceed your guests' expectations.

Chapter 3 Strategy Statement:

We recognize that our guests do not need to visit us, and they could do anything else with their time and money, and we appreciate that they chose to spend it with us.

Chapter 4:
Don't Put the Cart Before the Horse

once traveled to San Diego to visit a client and arrived at my hotel early in the morning, around 8:00 a.m. or so. When I entered the lobby, I observed three front desk agents, each assisting a guest at the counter, with no guests in line. Perfect. My expectation was that there would be a short wait, maybe twenty to thirty seconds at the most, since all three guests were checking out. Even when covering all of the necessary service points, the checkout process in a hotel is usually very quick.

After standing in line and waiting impatiently for more than four minutes, I was able to determine what their priorities were. All three agents I observed were incredibly friendly. They went far above and beyond what one would expect during a standard checkout. In fact, my observation was that they went *too* far. Yes, these employees were *so* friendly that the Hospitality Mentality backfired into an experience that was less than satisfactory. Outside of asking the questions needed for the functional logistics of the checkout, such as asking how their stay was, whether they needed a copy of their bill, or whether they needed assistance with luggage or transportation to the airport, they continued with questions like, "How was your business meeting?" "Did you get to any sightseeing while you were in town?" "Are you coming back to San Diego again anytime soon?" "Have you been here before?" "What are your kids doing this summer?" And more.

I stood there, amazed at the level of service they were providing, and thought, *This would be so much better if I wasn't here.* And that was the truth. With no guests in line, there is ample opportunity to extend the conversation with guests to create a truly personalized experience. However, these agents were all so busy making sure that they would exceed the "Friendliness" expectation, that the expectation of "Efficiency" took a backseat. By the time it was my turn to approach the desk and check in, a queue had formed behind me, and all of us were looking at each other saying, "It's great that they're friendly, but it would be even better if their friendliness didn't create a longer line for the rest of us." Rather, we expected that the agents would have aligned service and efficiency together by demonstrating their friendliness and urgency at the same time to keep the line moving. There are usually opportunities to personalize the experience during times of higher volumes of business, but these are best taken swiftly and while completing another necessary task. If it takes seven seconds to print out the guest's folio, then there are seven seconds that can be optimized to engage in further conversation, and then wrapped up quickly in order to show the guest that you are as committed to moving the queue as much as you are to providing great service. The same can be said when swiping a credit card, setting a plate down, retrieving merchandise, and several other tasks that can either be done in silence or improved with even a small amount of engagement. Personalizing the experience during busy times will be covered further in chapter 5.

In 2010, *Harvard Business Review* published a research study that showed that businesses were trying too hard. In the article titled "Stop Trying to Delight Your Customers," the authors highlighted the importance of simply meeting needs. "According to conventional wisdom, customers are more loyal to firms that go above and beyond. But our research shows that exceeding their expectations during service interactions (for example, by offering a refund, a free product, or a free service such as expedited shipping) makes customers only marginally more loyal than simply meeting their needs."[11] We will certainly cover strategies for going above and beyond, and how delighting your guests is an important driver of loyalty without using the word "free" or "refund," but the sequence in which you implement these strategies is linear, and when you try to delight your guests before *simply meeting their needs*, you are running a high risk of a failed guest experience.

The order in which you manage the guest experience is important. You have to walk before you can run, and you cannot start to think about exceeding your guests' expectations until you have focused on meeting them first. If you begin your day thinking about how you can take one of the expectations from the list and go above and beyond, you run the risk of neglecting one or more of the other expectations. What happens as a result is you inadvertently deliver the guest experience out of order. However, if you first identify what all the expectations are and make sure that they can be met, only then can you work toward putting together initiatives that exceed them. Think of the list of expectations as your hospitality checklist. You need to fulfill all of the components before you begin operations, and once you are up and running, you are still running through the list over the course of the day, making sure you are firing on all cylinders. If one is out of place, the rest can fall like dominoes.

Your guests expect that you will provide them with an experience that leaves them with a memory, and, as discussed in chapter 3, the experience is made up of multiple interwoven components that are required in order to meet guests' expectations. As we move on to what it means to meet guests' expectations, we must first confront the difficult challenge that lies ahead. There are two statements that were derived in the last chapter that are both true, yet they don't always agree with each other. The first is that **your expectation must be set so high that it exceeds the expectation of all possible alternatives**. This must happen simply in order to win the business in the first place. The second is that **in order to achieve guest loyalty, you must exceed your guests' expectations** at a bare minimum.

This is where promise meets delivery. The phrase "underpromise and overdeliver" is great when you are providing a need. The example I gave earlier of waiting in line to renew your driver's license comes to mind because when you think about it, the DMV actually has a substantial advantage over other industries. Historically, the DMV has developed such a poor reputation for long lines and poor efficiency that it doesn't take much for them to be able to exceed your expectations. They are usually the go-to punchline when telling a joke about poor service or efficiency. On the other hand, a hospitality business must promise a considerable amount just to be given the opportunity to even *attempt* to exceed the guest's expectation. As we have already determined, the deck is not stacked in our favor. It is not easy to exceed an expectation when it is intentionally set considerably high.

When determining what it means to meet your guests' expectations, consider the ways your guests can feel upon completing their experience. When you break it down to simple outcomes, each guest's postvisit sentiment toward your business can be categorized as one of the following three potentials:

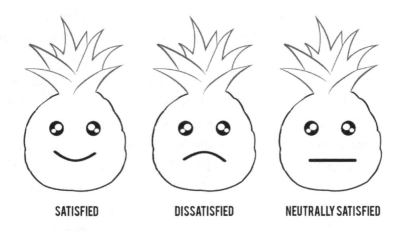

| SATISFIED | DISSATISFIED | NEUTRALLY SATISFIED |

If the guest is satisfied, congratulations! You have successfully exceeded their high expectation through the experience that you delivered. The guest sensed the Hospitality Mentality throughout their experience, and they are on their way to achieving loyalty status. If the guest is dissatisfied, it means that their experience fell below their expectation upon arrival, resulting in one or more service failures. It's not the end of the world, but you must work to win them back. And lastly, if the guest is neutrally satisfied, this would indicate that the expectation and the experience were identical, and you have therefore met the expectation exactly. Unless your guests tell you otherwise (either through voluntarily providing feedback or if they provide comments when prompted), you assume that guests fall into the third category as neutrally satisfied, and we need to examine that closer.

If you supposedly meet your guests' expectations directly, you have not achieved the goals that you should have set when it comes to the guest experience. This means that their experience was a transactional fulfillment of what they expected to pay for, nothing more and nothing less. That's customer service. While it could be argued that meeting guests' expectations is better than falling below, this also assumes a lack of guest feedback. While guest dissatisfaction will be discussed in greater detail in chapter 10, it is worth noting now that a dissatisfied guest who leaves your property without providing feedback falls into the classification of "neutrally satisfied" and can have significant negative impacts. They did not give you the opportunity to improve. This is the same with guests who supposedly had a positive experience that you don't know about. There is no indication of whether they will return or not, or whether they will influence others to visit through positive word of mouth. If you have no feedback, you assume neutral satisfaction, which is dangerous. While it may sound counterintuitive, it is more productive to attempt to push a neutrally satisfied guest into the realm of *dissatisfaction*, rather than allow them to remain in a neutral state. You can take action with dissatisfied guests in highly productive ways. A neutrally satisfied guest has little value to your organization unless you move them into either the camp of satisfied or dissatisfied. We will review these methods in chapter 9. The Hospitality Mentality makes no assumptions when it comes to guest satisfaction.

Additionally, the likelihood of the experience directly meeting the expectation head-on is minimal, if even possible at all. Your guests' expectations are very specific; they are made of components that can include a previous visit or experience, word of mouth from direct connections, reviews posted online from indirect connections, your marketing strategies, a sign that catches their eye as they drive by, a news segment, and more in-depth research. Pinpointing what exactly the guest expects is nearly impossible to do because of all of the factors that make it up. And if the expectation is specific and hard to define, so is the experience. The experience that each of your guests has will vary from one guest to the next, even if only slightly, due to a number of factors that include the time of day, day of the week, time of year that they visit, staff members with whom they interact, the weather, operational logistics, technical logistics, and many others that make the guest experience also hard to define and considered to be very narrow.

Factors that impact expectations	Factors that impact experience
Word of mouth	Time of day
Online reviews	Day of the week
Previous experience(s)	Time of year
Newspaper articles or media stories	Weather
Commercials and billboards	Specific interactions and experiences
Digital (web, social media, email marketing)	What's available or unavailable
Driving by	Gas prices and other external influence

This list is also not necessarily comprehensive of your specific business. I encourage you to use this list as a baseline to identify other factors that impact both expectations and experience. Based on the variety of factors that impact both expectations and experience, no two guests (or groups of guests) will have the exact same *expectation* prior to their visit, and no two guests (or groups of guests) will have the exact same *experience* during their visit. They may be very similar, but when breaking it down to the granular level, they are never exactly the same. This also means that because of how specific the expectations and experiences both are, they cannot be equal. Therefore, when we follow this logic, **neutral satisfaction does not exist**. Your guests will either be satisfied or dissatisfied, even if only slightly offset from the center, but the expectation cannot be met head-on. At this point, you are probably wondering why I felt that it was important to include an entire chapter on meeting guests' expectations if I don't believe in its existence. To answer this, let's quickly review the list of expectations from chapter 3 that make up the experience and the memory that you provide. Your guests expect that you will be some form of the following:

| SAFE | OPEN | EFFICIENT | CLEAN |

| WELL MAINTAINED | ENJOYABLE | FRIENDLY | AN ESCAPE |

Your Expectations Are Promises

The purpose of providing this list is not to elaborate on *how* to meet each of these expectations, given the specificity of each component and varying practices from one organization to the next. Instead, I present this graphic again to point out that these are promises that you are making to your guests. If the guest expects you to be open on time, it is because you have promised them that you will be open at the advertised time. You promised your guests that you will provide an environment that is clean and well maintained, and your guests expect that at a minimum. Each promise is an ongoing initiative, and these initiatives are never complete. If you are committed to exceeding your guests' expectations, you must first keep the promises that you've made.

As you merge this list with any additional expectations that are unique to your business, consider this as your guest experience checklist that must be accomplished before opening each day. You have promised these expectations in some shape or form, whether from your organization directly (i.e., through marketing) or through word of mouth, social media, or online reviews. And if you meet the promise, you have a chance of exceeding their expectations because you are setting the stage for a favorable guest experience. If your promises fall short of their delivery, you wind up with a service failure that leads to dissatisfaction. While broken promises are rarely intentional and in some cases are justifiable, they must still be recognized as a promise that could not be fulfilled, leading to a lackluster guest experience and a service failure.

Do → Tell → Show

When you look at expectations as promises, you gain a higher sense of responsibility. It's one thing to not live up to an expectation, but it's another thing to be known as someone who breaks a promise. People are spending their hard-earned money with you in exchange for some form of an experience, and that experience is made up of multiple factors and expectations that surround it. Because you have promised these expectations, you must first ensure that you are living up to the promises you've made, and *then* you can focus on delivering delightful elements of the experience that were unpromised, in the interest of exceeding expectations.

However, keeping your promises isn't enough. Guests today want to have a greater awareness of how your promises are being fulfilled in order to have full confidence in visiting. For instance, if you promise your guests an efficient experience during even the busiest of times, and as a result, you are staffed accordingly and running at full optimization, you've met the first requirement of keeping the promise. But if your guests aren't aware, it might negatively impact their perception if they observe a staff member who is not actively involved with the operation's efficiency, even if they are not tasked with that role and have no impact on it. Therefore, step one is to *do* what you promised, but it doesn't fulfill the kept promise that the guest expects.

The next step is then to *tell*, and ensure that guests are made aware, whether it is through verbal communication, signage, email, social media, on your website, or anywhere else that sends some sort of message of *Hey, we know it's busy, and we're working harder than ever to give you the experience you deserve.* If you've ever seen an overwhelming number of commercials around the holidays for Amazon, the postal service, or UPS, you can see that their core message is actively swaying you away from thinking, *Why is my package taking so long?* by telling you that they are in fact, hustling to come as close as possible to the speed that you expect.

Telling your guests how you keep your promises adds a bit more consumer confidence, but the third tier is to *show* your guests how you keep your promises. Continuing the efficiency example, allocating staff so that they are more visible in front-of-house areas will show guests that they are genuinely hustling, compared to if the staff's efforts could not be seen in plain sight. Sometimes, this step may require additional effort exerted, even if it is purely for the optics. If your staff is speaking loudly and at a slightly more rapid pace, it gives the appearance that they are moving faster, even if the work can be done just as efficiently at a normal volume and tone. Anything that you can do to amplify the promise that is within view of your guests will regularly drive the point home that you are keeping the promise you made, and therefore, meeting their expectations. Tactical elements like this will be discussed in greater detail in the bonus content, to which you will find the details in the conclusion.

The best way to ensure guests know that you are keeping your promises is by doing a combination of *do, tell, show* on a regular basis, and with each of the expectations. As you review the list of expectations along with any additional ones that you add to it, consider how you can implement a sense of *do, tell, show* with each of them.

For safety, how many safety procedures are done in front of guests to demonstrate that their safety is your top priority?

During operating hours, does the facility or venue feel welcome and open, or will guests second-guess themselves upon arrival?

For efficiency, is your staff visibly working to move guests through each area of the guest journey, even if the volume of business is higher than average, and therefore, might run slower than during an off-peak time?

Are you demonstrating your cleanliness standard in front of guests by actively picking up trash, cleaning and sanitizing, and demonstrating proper hygiene?

Are maintenance issues addressed quickly and in front of guests when necessary, so that guests can observe your commitment to keeping a well-maintained facility?

Do staff members proactively approach guests with a friendly greeting and offer of assistance, rather than waiting to be approached?

Does your environment reflect an enjoyable experience through atmosphere and ambiance, including lighting, music, and landscaping?

Can escapism be sensed in that the guest has crossed a threshold that leaves behind the less glamorous elements of real life?

To expand on the final point of escapism, you do not need to transport your guests to another world to show them the sense of escapism, but you can bring them a few steps closer by looking at your operation through the lens of the guest who wants to feel like they have entered somewhere "different." This involves small steps, like hiding loose cables from electronics and removing clutter behind a desk, or taking things that feel too "administrative" or office-like out of view. This is the case in a coffee shop or a dry cleaner as much as it is in a fully immersive experience. These are not end-of-the-world distractions, but an unremarkable environment for an otherwise transformative experience is too much of a clash between the real world and the world that your guests are entering. Take note of all of the "regular" things that can be found in front of house and see what you can eliminate or move back of house, all in the interest of escapism.

You Can't Compromise on Safety, But You Can Still Meet Your Other Promises

It can be argued that *safety* is the one expectation that does not need to work in tandem with the rest, and you are afforded the flexibility to forgo the other promises if concern for safety ever arises. While this is true to some extent, the remainder of the promises must still be acknowledged. They may take a different form, but they are all still present in the mix of the overall operation and guest experience. Once, while I was on a flight from Atlanta to Chicago, the pilot suffered a medical emergency and the plane was diverted to Indianapolis, the nearest major city, and we made an emergency landing late at night. This resulted in passengers being stranded overnight in a city that was not their final destination, with ongoing ambiguities as to what the next developments were in relation to our continuation home. Getting the pilot to medical care without compromising the safety of the plane, passengers, or the crew was the ultimate priority.

Had the airline seen safety as the only promise that needed to be met, this would have excused them from urgently seeking a new flight crew, accommodating guests in hotels upon determining there was no crew that could safely or legally fly, or ensuring that the flight took off again at the reassigned time. Instead, every staff member stayed in constant communication with passengers, starting on the plane when the emergency landing was announced, once on the ground after the pilot was taken off, and after deplaning while passengers waited patiently in the gate area. The staff kept us informed every step of the way and did so in a professional manner, which protected the promises of friendliness and efficiency. The flight crew kept the promise of cleanliness by picking up the trash that was left on the aircraft after we deplaned because they were unable to do a final sweep before the plane landed. Ultimately, they strived to maintain as many of the expectations as they could while still seeing to it that the pilot was transported to receive medical attention, therefore ensuring that the safety of the pilot, the passengers, and the crew was the highest priority. There was a procedure in place that enabled all of their promises to be met given the significant shift in circumstance, and never compromising safety.

An expectation like safety is one that cannot be compromised, and more recently, cleanliness has taken on that role as well. Therefore, one might assume that if you only focus on safety, or on safety and cleanliness, the remainder of the expectations do not need to apply. When businesses began to reopen when restrictions were lifted from the COVID-19 pandemic, it was apparent which businesses amplified their focus on safety and cleanliness, showing that they were the top priorities for guests and staff members alike. You may recall that this was not the case for other businesses, and those that fell below were either forced to close or quickly revamp how they managed their procedures, while at the same being exposed on social media in real time.

The businesses that walked this line the best though were those that amplified their safety and cleanliness procedures due to physical distancing and concerns with high contact touchpoints while blending in the remainder of their guest expectations and modifying them so that they could still meet the expectations that guests always had, which would then allow the opportunity to exceed them. Once safety and cleanliness procedures were updated, one of the expectations that was most at risk was efficiency. When businesses needed to reduce capacity, clean more frequently, and enforce physical distancing within their premises, it made it more challenging to operate at efficiency levels even close to what they were previously. It took creative initiatives to look at the full list of guest expectations and determine how meeting each expectation needed to be modified.

For example, let's examine how a retail store that previously would allow shoppers to enter and exit at their leisure would not need to worry about how many shoppers were in the store at any given time unless it approached maximum occupancy which would result in a fire hazard (which would only be an issue on very rare occurrences, and usually easy to anticipate if projected visitation was in place and mostly accurate). Once reopening, their capacities were drastically reduced due to physical distancing. While it wouldn't compromise standards from a fire safety standpoint, shoppers within the store needed to maintain ample distance from each other.

This often resulted in a new position of a greeter positioned outside the entrance, who needed to maintain full control of the exact number of shoppers within the store. While shoppers lined up outside the store, they were allowed inside in a one in, one out fashion, so the capacity would never be exceeded. Once inside, perhaps it was business as usual if shoppers were to casually browse merchandise and meander. The best greeters, however, would prevent that from happening because the dwell time in the store would have to be cut down drastically, otherwise, efficiency would be out the window. Guests waiting in line outside the store would become frustrated, potentially leave the line, or prospective shoppers walking by would decide not to shop. All three of these outcomes are not ideal, and the second and third would result in loss of revenue, which was so badly needed for a brick-and-mortar business.

The greeter could manage this by striking up a conversation with the next shopper in line, which would meet the expectation of friendliness, but also ascertain crucial information. If a shopper needed a specific item, the greeter was able to use their proficiency to say where exactly in the store it is, reducing browsing time significantly. If an item was out of stock, the greeter could tell the shopper upfront, resulting in them leaving the line—again, this would not be ideal, but it would be better to prevent the shopper from taking time within the store only to find that they couldn't make a purchase and then focus on the next shopper behind them. If a shopper was making a return, the greeter could make sure that they have all the necessary information and proof of purchase, and then make sure that they get to the register right away. By combining these elements of service and efficiency, the store would be able to effectively provide a safe and clean environment that shoppers felt comfortable entering, while also ensuring a satisfactory experience from a service standpoint, and ultimately, as efficient of an operation as possible.

When you view the list of expectations as your ongoing to-do list, you focus on checking the items off the list before adding new items to the list. And because each component is dynamic and ever-changing over the course of each and every day, the list is not completed when you open the doors for the day. Before coming up with creative ways to exceed your guests' expectations, you must first make sure that they can be met. Even though the expectation and the experience will each vary from one guest to the next, holding each of your promises with the highest regard will pave the way for you to most successfully exceed expectations, and then use that satisfaction to convert it to loyalty. And it all starts with meeting expectations, doing things in the right order, and not putting the cart before the horse.

Chapter 4 Strategy Statement:

We seek to meet expectations before we exceed them and keep the promises that we've made.

PART 2:

EXCEED THE EXPECTATION

W alt Disney once said, "You can design and create, and build the most wonderful place in the world. But it takes people to make the dream a reality."[12] I believe this quote is so powerful because Walt in fact did, according to much of the general public, design, create, and build the most wonderful place in the world. However, this statement is so incredible because he did not suggest that the rides, shows, and characters would be the driving force of how to realize the vision, despite the company's ongoing commitment to unmatched show quality. Walt knew quite well that it was the frontline cast who would make or break whether this dream of his would become a reality or just another venue that offered some sort of entertainment. That was quite a gamble, but this quote from Walt Disney is a textbook example of the Hospitality Mentality.

This quote applies just the same to you too. Whatever type of business you are in, even if your facility is magnificent, well maintained, clean, and designed creatively, it is worth nothing if the human beings who are delivering the experience to other human beings are not on top of their game because the experience will never exceed the expectation. This is one of the many reasons why the Hospitality Mentality is widely applicable across industries and types of business. Regardless of whether you classify what you do as businesses-to-business or business-to-consumer, we are all in the same business of human-to-human. Even when your product may speak for itself, the driving force behind the product is what results in higher than average satisfaction, repeat business or purchases, positive word of mouth, and of course the endgame we are all trying to reach, lifelong loyalty.

This is the **moment of truth**. This is where the rubber meets the road and the expectation (made up of your promises) is put to the test. This refers to every interaction that your guests have with some element of your product, and especially the elements that are largely within your control: the human element of the employees that deliver the experience. There is not just one moment of truth that needs to be considered; there are many. The moments of truth may begin before their visit if they make a phone call or send an email to inquire about information or if they see your social media team in action online. It then leads into the arrival process, and into their experience with every staff member with whom they interact over the course of their visit. It extends beyond their visit as they continue to engage with your brand in the postvisit phase of the guest experience cycle. Every interaction is a moment of truth. That means that every interaction is an opportunity to exceed guests' expectations. Although, at the same time, it means that every interaction is a risk of a service failure as well. Ultimately, you have a choice every single time. For every single guest interaction, you have the ability to determine whether the interaction will exceed or fall below guests' expectations. And upon conclusion of the visit, the guest will have this collection of interactions, or "moments of truth," that will ultimately determine how satisfied they are with their experience.

What Does Going Above and Beyond Look Like?

Using the human element as the core for how to exceed your guests' expectations, we will review the most effective ways that you and your staff can take the guest experience to the next level. This section will cover the following:

- **Chapter 5: Deliver a Hyperpersonalized Experience:** how to make each guest feel like they are the only ones who matter, and how to use that skill to increase revenue
- **Chapter 6: Be More Enthusiastic than Your Guests:** avoid mundane repetition, even when requiring a routine to carry out the job duties most effectively
- **Chapter 7: Anticipate Guests' Needs:** use a combination of proficiency and awareness to offer an experience that is better than the guest anticipated
- **Chapter 8: Make an Impact with "Wow" Moments:** take the guest experience to the next level by providing moments that surprise and delight

Chapter 5:
Deliver a Hyperpersonalized Experience

In downtown Atlanta, Georgia Aquarium is ranked as one of the top visitor attractions in the city, and one of its biggest highlights is its dolphin presentation. Guests are often blown away by the sheer size of the theater, the majesty of the dolphins, and the production quality of the entertainment that this show, which runs multiple times daily, provides. Therefore, one might think that with so many guests sitting in a crowded theater for a show that is exactly the same whether you see it at 11:00 a.m., 1:00 p.m., 3:00 p.m., or next Tuesday, it must be impossible to personalize the experience. The staff at Georgia Aquarium think otherwise. They take on the challenge of delivering a personalized experience in what would otherwise seem to be an impersonal environment.

When I had the opportunity to see this presentation, I arrived at the theater about fifteen to twenty minutes before the presentation started. I took a seat near the top of the stadium, allowing for a full panoramic view. As guests were entering to take their seats, they were greeted by an usher, who was available for questions along with any assistance required. Once inside the theater, another member of the team was present, and equipped with a microphone, allowing him to pump up the crowd and bring high energy to the room in anticipation of the presentation starting.

While chatting with guests, making jokes, and keeping the crowd entertained, he came across a small child sitting in one of the first few rows who was wearing a button signaling that it was her birthday. Seeing an opportunity to use his power of influence at that moment (as in, a microphone and an audience), he drew attention to the girl and her birthday button and asked what her name was and how old she was turning. She replied that her name was Kayla and she was turning six years old.

A positive experience would have been to wish Kayla a happy birthday and thank her for celebrating at the aquarium. Maybe even offer a high five if he was close enough. But instead, he directed his attention to the audience and asked all of us to join in by singing "Happy Birthday" to this young guest. Full of enthusiasm, he began counting, "1 . . . 2 . . . 3 . . ." and the entire audience delivered a beautiful serenade. Everyone in the crowd was positively impacted by this experience, but no one was more excited than Kayla. While there were hundreds of guests congregating in that theater, for that one moment, Kayla was the only one who mattered. And that personal experience was crafted in the moment to last forever.

It seems too often that personalization of service is inversely proportional to the success of the business. The more successful you become, the more guests there are to serve, and the less of an opportunity there is to deepen the relationship with your guests. Less chitchat. Get them in, get them out, and move on to the next. Be consistent. Be efficient. Don't do anything that will disrupt the machine-like operation of your business. That is why this chapter is the first step in exceeding guests' expectations, to prove that being successful or even busy does not excuse you from delivering a hyperpersonalized experience to as many guests as possible. As we know, every moment of truth is an opportunity to exceed expectations, and going above and beyond must be a personal experience in order to create a memory that lasts longer than the experience itself.

When looking to deliver a hyperpersonalized experience, we can break it down into four primary components:

1. Learn and use the guest's name
2. Extend the conversation beyond the functional needs
3. Make the guest feel as if they are the only one who matters
4. Customize recommendations that match the uniqueness of each guest

Learn and Use the Guest's Name

Nothing is more personal than using someone's name in conversation. By actively learning your guests' names and showing them that you remember them, it extends the interaction beyond transactional—beyond *customer* service—and you begin to build rapport with the individual. Using your guests' names can be the difference between providing a four-star experience and a five-star.

Extend the Conversation Beyond Functional Needs

Most service providers are running through a checklist in their minds that, when completed, ensures a consistent experience. While consistency is necessary for meeting expectations, going beyond the expectation means going beyond the checklist and extending interactions toward seeking commonalities whenever possible.

Make the Guest Feel as if They Are the Only One Who Matters

Even in a sea of people during times of peak business, seek opportunities to provide individual attention to guests when possible, and when it can be done without neglecting any of the other expectations. When the guest feels that they are the only one who matters, it amplifies their connection with the business.

Customize Recommendations that Match the Uniqueness of Each Guest

While you can't always create a new offering, menu item, or package that will meet the specific needs of every individual you interact with, you can align the reasoning behind specific offerings that resonate with the guest, in which they feel that it was created just for them. This leads to more than a feel-good feeling for the guest; it can actually increase their spending.

In the major theme parks in Central Florida, one of the biggest complaints that guests will make during peak season is that, in addition to the extensive crowds, they feel like they are being "herded like cattle" through queues and experiences, which indicates that the operators are more concerned about throughput and efficiency during this time of the year than they are about providing an enjoyable experience. This is the opposite side of the coin compared to the problem I presented in chapter 4 when the hotel's front desk agents were so friendly that it made the line longer, where efficiency was secondary to service. When these complaints are expressed in the theme parks, guests perceive that the staff is *so* focused on efficiency that it actually deteriorates the experience, and that personalized service is seen to be less of a priority. What is initially thought to be well-intentioned operations in an effort to minimize wait times, actually results in guests constantly feeling like they need to keep moving, otherwise they would be left behind. In my hotel example in chapter 4, I was upset that the staff was too friendly, and in Orlando at Christmastime, guests complain that the staff is trying to be too efficient. It's a lose-lose conundrum!

This presents the challenge of how to create a personalized experience for as many guests as possible, even during times when the volume of business is higher than average. The answer resides in understanding that there are a wide variety of options for personalizing an interaction that serves the full spectrum of what is suitable for any given situation. Smaller crowds or slower seasons lend themselves to longer interactions with more staff members. During higher volumes of business, you generally cannot engage in a lengthy conversation, but there are small pockets of time during nearly every interaction that allow you to still personalize that interaction, even if you aren't necessarily going to become best friends. "Is this your first time here?" or "Are you from nearby?" are quick and easy questions that allow the guest to talk about themselves, but they don't require further investigation if the time does not permit. However, it can also be expanded to "What brought you here today?" or "How's the weather back home?" The guest is offered the opportunity to continue talking about themselves, and it shows that they are going a little beyond what they expected from the interaction.

People frequently have conversation starters on them that indicate where they are from, what school they attend (or attended), which sports teams hold their allegiance, where they get their coffee, or which movies, bands, or television shows they like. Take note of how guests are bringing their personalities with them through hats, shirts, jackets, coffee cups, hairstyles, or otherwise presented as a distinct feature. These are perfect conversation pieces that can serve the full spectrum of interactions. Quick acknowledgments of these items, even in passing, show the guest that you care, and even if efficiency is the top priority at the time, these quick moments do not occupy enough time to slow down the operation. When the opportunity permits, asking further questions about their hometown, school, or sports team, again, allows the guest to talk about themselves while you show that you are interested in them. For sports teams, you do not have to be a fan of the team to acknowledge that the guest is (as long as it doesn't turn into a rivalry feud—I've seen it happen). If you are up to date with anything related to what you recognize the guest might be interested in, an opportunity exists to personalize the interaction. Even if you are not up to date, ask questions! Who won that game last night? Where is that school located? What genre of music does this band play? Asking someone to talk about their favorite subject or something that they are passionate about is a surefire way to generate a moment of satisfaction.

This goes beyond logoed apparel. Picking up on cues from what the guest might be saying, even in passing, can lead to a personalized interaction. While visiting a museum once, I made an observation that two exhibits had switched places since my last visit, which gave the cue that I had visited previously. This opened up the conversation for the staff member to inquire about my past visits, confirm that I live locally, and then discuss the benefits of membership (this will be discussed in greater detail later in this chapter).

The Power of Names

The most challenging yet often the most impactful method of personalizing the guest experience involves obtaining and using the guest's name throughout the conversation. This is much more difficult during peak times, but in opportunities when it can be achieved, it takes the guest experience to the next level. If the guest is required to show their identification, you have their name. If the guest pays with a credit card, you have their name. If you are tuned in to conversations and overhear names being used, you have their name. Also, if you introduce yourself and ask for their name in return, you are amplifying the personalization of the interaction and the overall experience. When you use the guest's name in conversation, you demonstrate that they are not just another transaction or another guest that needs to be "herded through," but that they are truly a guest that you have invested even a little bit of time in. When you're given the opportunity, here is a challenge for you: try to use the guest's name at least three times in conversation. You will quickly see how this elevates the guest experience, and it costs nothing to do it.

Use the Basics to Focus Your Attention

When you deliver a genuinely personalized experience, you make your guests feel as if they are the only ones who matter at that moment. The moment may be brief or lengthy, depending on the nature of the interaction, but during that time, the focus is on them. This is equally applicable to being proactive or reactive with every guest interaction. When looking at basic expectations of guest service, including smiling, making eye contact, not using a phone, not crossing your arms, and not leaning, it is most productive to align these requirements with the purpose. Each of these small gestures individually makes up what becomes a personalized experience, and doing the opposite is exactly that: an impersonal interaction. Maintaining eye contact shows that you are free from distractions and fully focused, meaning that the guest in front of you is the only one who matters. Physical gestures, such as crossing your arms, demonstrate a more reserved personality that makes you less approachable. All of these rules might be in your playbook or employee manual, but are they presented as "do this or else" rules, or are they presented as "these are some of the tools to deliver a personal experience"? Having your hands in your pockets does not make someone a bad employee and certainly not a bad person, but it does come across as less personable. Make sure your staff is not only aware of the rules, but the reasons why these guidelines are in place. Then, instead of laying down the law on what *not* to do, provide your staff with the tools and direction for what they *can* do instead, which can lead to greater levels of employee satisfaction due to feeling more fulfilled, rather than doing their best to not break the rules.

Personalizing guest interactions may seem like a "soft skill," one that's nice to use when it's possible. It makes guests happier when put into practice, and it might seem like there won't be a negative impact if it's not done. Guests may not directly say or think, "I wish the staff would have used my name in conversation a little more," or "I can't believe they didn't point out my baseball cap, even though my team just won the World Series." In the vast majority of circumstances, guests might not have this on their minds. However, when you increase the number of personalized interactions, the net result is a heightened guest experience, leading to higher satisfaction upon departure. In these cases, your guests' reactions will include statements that not only relate to their experience, but also to the individuals who made it spectacular. This is why offering a hypersonalized experience exceeds expectations and offers an experience that is heightened compared to the already high standard that the guest expects upon arrival.

The beginning of this chapter started with a story from Georgia Aquarium, which is frequently recognized for its outstanding guest service, and examples like the one I shared can be found all over. Keeping it in the zoo and aquarium family, but this time one in New Orleans, let's see how personalizing the guest experience results in Tripadvisor reviews like this one:[13]

Awesome Experience!

Review of Audubon Zoo

●●●●● Reviewed August 10, 2017

I had some difficulties purchasing tickets for the Backstage Penguin Pass due to web site maintenance. I called and spoke with a very friendly lady who took my information and called me as soon as the web site was back up! That's what I call excellent customer service!

My girlfriend and I had an awesome experience at the Backstage Penguin Pass! We found Tom to be extremely friendly and knowledgeable about the penguins as well as the Audubon Zoo. His passion for educating visitors and his deep love for the animals was heartwarming and genuine. And of course, we can't forget the REAL start of the show - "Elmyr"! She was a sweet little penguin and we are desperately hoping that she will get to stay there at Audubon and not sent to another zoo!

Reviews like the one here demonstrate that when the guest feels like they are the only ones who matter at that moment, that feeling of exclusivity is what resonates far beyond the conclusion of their experience. And it gets better. In this particular case, this review highlights a premium experience that is substantially more expensive than general admission to the aquarium. Guests who are considering what to do as they are planning their trip to New Orleans might decide whether the aquarium is worth it or not. When they stumble across this review, due to the personal level of attention that this guest received during their visit, not only will prospective visitors see this as a benefit of visiting the aquarium, but now they have increased awareness of the value of the Backstage Penguin Pass. Even if they don't book it in advance, if a staff member recommends it upon arrival or at any point during their visit, this review acts as the social proof of why they should book it, and ultimately spend the extra money. This leads me to my next important point.

Personalizing the Guest Experience Is a Revenue Growth Strategy

A personalized experience can and should lead to higher guest spending, meaning that this is not just a service strategy, but it crosses over into sales as well. Committing a designated moment for each guest, no matter how brief of an interaction, can influence them to purchase more, upgrade, or enhance their experience. You and your staff possess the proficiency of your business, your operations, and the variety of ways to experience it, and when this proficiency collides with the desire to assist a guest in a personal way, it drives revenue. Let's use the example of Audubon's premium experience, the Backstage Penguin Pass, as indicated in the Tripadvisor review just presented.

The fictional, but realistic, scenario goes as follows: I read that review while determining what to do when visiting New Orleans, and while that one review may not have been the ultimate determining factor, it made me feel good about the choice I made because I wanted to visit the aquarium anyway. I saw that there is this penguin experience and noticed that that's what this guest did because they mentioned it in their review, but I have not put much more thought into it, nor do I even really know what it is. In my mind, I am going to purchase one general admission ticket to the aquarium for each member of my family.

When I arrive at the aquarium at around 10:30 a.m., I am greeted at the box office by a friendly staff member who is smiling and making eye contact when I walk up to the window. This interaction might look something like this:

ADMISSIONS TEAM MEMBER: Hi, welcome to Audubon Aquarium! My name is Karen. And you are?
ME: I'm Josh. Glad to be here!
KAREN: Me too! Where are you visiting from, Josh?

ME: We're in town from Chicago.

KAREN: Nice! You have a great aquarium up there too. Now, Josh, have you been to Audubon before?

ME: Nope, first time here!

KAREN: Well, let me be the first to welcome you. I'm so glad you're here, Josh. How long are you visiting New Orleans?

ME: This is actually our last day in town. Heading home tomorrow.

KAREN: Ahh, well, I'm glad you made it here before you headed back home! Since you only have one day left in town, I want to make sure you have the best possible experience with us. Josh, do you like penguins? Or better yet, have you ever met one before?

ME: Met a penguin? I can't say that I have!

KAREN: Josh, I'm going to let you in on a little secret. You can visit the aquarium and have an amazing experience seeing all of our exhibits, but because you came all the way from Chicago to visit us, I want to make sure you make the most of your time here. *(Karen then leans in toward me and speaks with a softer voice, without breaking eye contact.)* You and your family could have a more intimate experience where you get to hang out with the penguins in a much smaller group. From personal experience, I can tell you that it is absolutely worth it. If you want, Josh, I can check to see what times we have available today. It tends to sell out a lot, so I can see what we have left.

At this point, I might remember, at least to some extent, the Tripadvisor review I read that raved about the service Tom provided during the Backstage Penguin Pass experience, and of course the penguin they met. Do I get to see for myself how amazing Tom is and how passionate he is about the animals? These are all the thoughts running through my head right now. Now, is it going to guarantee the sale? Of course not, and ultimately the guest will be the one to decide whether they see the value being presented.

But because of this heightened awareness due to the personal attention that Karen provided, the odds of making the sale are notably higher. At the time of this writing, there is approximately a $90 difference in cost between general admission at Audubon Aquarium and the Backstage Penguin Pass. Estimating an average party size of three guests, this $270 boost in revenue can happen multiple times daily. If this successfully results in a transaction only three times a day per admissions employee, then each staff member will produce nearly $300,000 annually in incremental revenue, *in addition to all other ticket sales!*

In this example, Karen was able to personalize the experience for me at that moment, and because she got me talking about myself, she gained crucial information that led to her making a recommendation, and the recommendation was just as personal as the rest of the conversation. She also obtained my name immediately and used it multiple times over the course of the interaction, showing that she had a genuine interest in me and that I wasn't just the next guest in line. The questions she asked were strategic too. If my answers had been different, the recommendation may have been different too. If I'd told her that I was in town for a week, she would have the chance to suggest the Audubon Experience Ticket, another premium option that would give me access to the aquarium *and* the zoo, which I may or may not have known about depending on the amount of research I did in advance or which Tripadvisor reviews I read.

Notice the way that she phrased the offering too, and why personalizing this interaction was so important. Instead of asking these questions and then making suggestions, she used the answers that I gave her to help build her response. This level of service would not have been achieved if Karen just showed up to work, clocked in, focused on checking off the boxes of what she was required to ask, sold some tickets, went home, and came back and did it again the next day. Instead, she determined that she was going to boost her guest interactions, not herd guests into the aquarium like cattle, and take the extra few seconds to make the arrival experience even more enjoyable. The cash register agreed with her approach. She also created the bridge that allowed me to cross from purchasing a general admission ticket to an option that was $90 more expensive and do so seamlessly and easily. She gave me a reason why I should choose this option, and it was never presented in the form of a question. She never asked, "Would you be interested in . . . ?" Instead, she told me what she recommended and why she recommended it, and the reason why had everything to do with me.

It is important to note the distinction between personalizing the experience and upselling. Upselling is a sales tactic and very transaction-focused, which involves pairing items that go well together in the interest of driving per capita spending (e.g., *Would you like fries with that?*). You may notice that there were minimal, if any, active sales techniques that occurred over the course of that dialogue. Instead, Karen conducted a hyperfocused market research study, where she collected demographic information and consumer habits and preferences, and then tailored a recommendation that maintained the level of personalization from the start. Karen made it seem like the Backstage Penguin Pass was created just for me out of thin air, and if I had any skepticism or lack of clarity from reading the review on Tripadvisor, I now felt more personally connected to this premium experience.

The made-up example provided here is based on an interaction with the sales associate, which makes sense because there is a direct tie-in with the potential revenue generated from the interaction. Although, revenue growth is not exclusively tied to those who are responsible for processing the transaction. For staff members in non-revenue-generating departments or positions, this can and should also be a natural part of the job description. Your staff should become proficient with all available offerings, especially where guests have the chance to enhance their experience, and they should weave these into conversations with guests regularly and where applicable and when relevant. Even if they are not the ones who will sell the experience, communicating the value of why the guest might consider this option will increase awareness. Think of it as on-site marketing, merged with guest service, fueled by personalizing the experience.

Let's connect this back with the efficiency concern, and not wanting to fall back on the promise of efficiency while going above and beyond with friendliness; it reduces satisfaction because it negatively impacts the experience of other guests. If Karen and I started chitchatting and went out of the scope of what was relevant for the transaction, it would be a disservice to the guests waiting in line behind me. This would have turned into the hotel check-in experience I had when the staff members focused so much on friendliness that they failed to keep other promises that guests expected. You may have even thought that this type of interaction is too time-consuming while you read the dialogue, and while it might work well on a slow day and when there are no other guests waiting in line, peak times of the day would dictate that the staff move the line and expedite the number of transactions per hour.

This strategy of processing transactions quicker will certainly move the line quicker, but it will not optimize the value of each guest. Notice how Karen controlled the conversation in the dialogue. She knew the questions she wanted to ask me—those that had definitive answers—and while it got me to open up a little, she was always in the driver's seat. She could have expanded or contracted that conversation as necessary, as the current queue dictated, and how much available time she knew she had with me. If the goal was to upsell, then it would have looked something like this when I walked up to the window:

> **KAREN:** Hi, welcome to Audubon Aquarium! How can I help you?
> **ME:** Two adults, one child.
> **KAREN:** Great! Would you like to do the Backstage Penguin Pass today?
> **ME:** No, thanks. Just general admission.
> **KAREN:** Okay. Your total will be *(brief pause as Karen rings in the transaction)* $80.
> **ME:** Here you go. *(I hand Karen my credit card.)*
> **KAREN:** All set! Here are your tickets, and the entrance is to your right. Have a great time!

This would probably take about half the time as the previous interaction when Karen personalized the experience. However, a slight increase in transaction time that yields a notably larger transaction size will increase both the value of the transaction along with guest satisfaction. This is where service and sales collide, with efficiency driving the flow of the operation. All of this can be achieved when you deliver a hyperpersonalized experience to every guest.

Delivering a hyperpersonalized experience is one of the most impactful ways to exceed expectations and build a rapport with your guests. This is presented as the first chapter in this section intentionally, as it allows you to forgo the customer-centric mentality and replace it with the Hospitality Mentality, in which you no longer have customers, but rather guests who will walk away with a perception of their experience that is disconnected from their transaction; when done effectively, a personalized experience will increase the transaction size, even without focusing on the transaction itself, because you present the best option for the guest in front of you and align it with their goals. The guest is seeking satisfaction from their own experience just as much as you are seeking to deliver it, and through these techniques, every guest can feel like they are the only one who matters, even if only for a brief moment, and at multiple points across the experience.

Chapter 5 Strategy Statement:

We aim to deliver a personalized experience at every possible opportunity, where the guest feels that they are the only one who matters, even if only for a brief moment.

Chapter 6:
Be More Enthusiastic than Your Guests

A ski instructor in the Swiss Alps. A docent at the Louvre. A skydiving instructor in New Zealand. A scuba trainer in the Bahamas. A helicopter pilot in Hawaii. A tour guide at the Vatican. What do these professions all have in common? For starters, they all have pretty enviable jobs. They get to see and do things every day that are considered once-in-a-lifetime experiences for the vast majority of the world's population. More importantly, the people they interact with are the ones *having* a once-in-a-lifetime experience. Their guests invest so much into saving and planning for these types of excursions that they *better* get the experience they expect, and absolutely nothing less.

Think about the disparity between the providers of these experiences and the participants. The size of the gap is incredible. These activities occur every single day (barring a pandemic that halts everything fun), and there are so many people who are living and breathing these lifestyles, yet so many of us will live our entire lives never knowing most of these incredible experiences. The normality of daily life includes waking up, going to work or school, running errands, eating a few times, watching television, going back to sleep, and then doing it again the next day. Those who work in these professions have similar routines, but their work seems so much more glamorous.

Now let's focus on what you do. Are you in any of these occupations? If so, I look forward to your invitation. But regardless of what the service is that you provide, consider the gap mentioned between how often you get to do what you do and how often your guests do it. Maybe you also fall into the once-in-a-lifetime category for your guests, or maybe your guests are much more frequent visitors. Whichever it is, take a look at the components of what you provide and consider how often they are experienced by your guests throughout their lifetime, whether it is while they visit you or even while visiting a competitor that offers a similar experience. What's the gap?

This chapter walks through how we address that gap. It starts with recognizing that the things that are normal for us are special for those we serve, and then showing the guest that we recognize the gap through our actions. To do this, you must be *more enthusiastic than your guests*, even when your guests' enthusiasm level is high.

Here are the four steps to maintain enthusiasm to the point where it is even higher than that of your guests:

1. Recognize the excitement level of your guests
2. Don't let the novelty wear off
3. Break from the routine whenever possible
4. Don't let the job become redundant

Recognize the Excitement Level of Your Guests

Take a look at the emotional expressions of your guests as you observe them experiencing what you have to offer. Is it awe?

Wonder? Surprise? Suspense? In order to act more enthusiastic than your guests, consider the baseline that you need to meet so that your excitement continues to lift theirs up.

Don't Let the Novelty Wear Off
No matter what you do, it is likely to be different from what the majority of your guests do. To that end, what is novel for them may be ordinary for you. That's perfectly fine and even expected, yet it takes intentional practice to recognize the novelty of the experience you're offering to your guests, and allow yourself to bring it back for you too.

Break from the Routine Whenever Possible
The previous chapter focused on going beyond the checklist or the functional mechanics of the job to ensure a personalized experience. By continuing to extend past the routine, you allow yourself to keep the experience fresh, and it enables you to creatively try new things that go beyond guests' expectations. Some may work better than others, but the important thing is to keep things fresh for yourself.

Don't Let the Job Become Redundant
By taking each of these steps, your work environment remains fresh and exciting, even in an operation that thrives on consistency. If your consistent routine also includes *breaking* from the routine, you create success for yourself to avoid redundancy in the way you deliver the routine. If things start to get boring, it's time to shake things up.

To expand on the final point, being more enthusiastic than your guests is largely about minimizing the feeling of redundancy in your work, regardless of how repetitive it may feel. To implement this strategy, I ask (and challenge you to ask your staff): what excited you about your business on your first day on the job, or perhaps prior to your employment if you visited as a guest? Essentially, what part of the guest experience was so exciting that is now part of your daily life? Maybe this aspect has become regular, routine, and perhaps even redundant. First of all, it's *okay* that it has reached the point of redundancy. The things we see every day might start to seem repetitive. But if you felt enthusiasm toward this aspect at the beginning, it's likely that your guests feel the same way, whether it is their first visit or the reason that they continue visiting. The novelty that you provide has not worn off on them.

This does not apply only to the professions mentioned at the beginning of the chapter, or to other life-changing experiences. If you're a barista, what are the unique coffee concoctions that you serve that your guests don't get to experience at other coffee shops? What are the unique elements of what you provide that make up the reasons why guests visit? Consider the question presented in chapter 3 that asked, what do your guests expect when they visit you? This helps develop the framework for predicting your guests' enthusiasm. If we were to go deeper into that question alone, we expand into the following follow-up questions:

- What do your guests get excited about when they visit?
- What drives their ultimate decision to visit?
- What are you known for?
- What do guests get upset about when they can't experience something during their visit?
- What/who are your guests taking selfies with?
- What are your guests posting on social media?

- When they come back, what do they do on every visit?
- What do (or what would you) put on a billboard to drive up demand to visit?

Maintaining Enthusiasm at 93 Mph

My first job out of high school was as a ride operator at Cedar Point in Sandusky, Ohio. I was fortunate to be on the ride crew at Millennium Force, a 310-foot roller coaster that travels at speeds of ninety-three miles per hour. While it opened in the year 2000, Millennium Force is still ranked as one of the top coasters on the planet, and coaster enthusiasts come from all over the world to experience it, along with the rest of the park's unmatched collection of thrills. The ride opened five years before I spent my first summer there, which was plenty of time for it to solidify its place as my favorite roller coaster, considering I visited the park as a guest countless times before that and happily waited in line, sometimes for two or even three hours, just to experience the two minutes of pure adrenaline. As a season passholder and superfan of the park as a teenager, I was a loyal guest—though I never hosted lasagna dinners for the crew like Pam did. As a high school student living 130 miles away, I made it my mission to get a summer job there right when I could, long before I realized that I desired my career to be in the theme parks and attractions industry.

When I was given the opportunity to be a ride operator, specifically at Millennium Force, I was thrilled! Being able to see guests' reactions all day as they got on and off would have been plenty of motivation for me to show up every day, but the icing on the cake was what happened every morning. Before opening, each ride vehicle needed to be test-ridden by a ride operator before the ride could open for the public. The purpose isn't for fun, but to look and listen for anything out of the ordinary. Not everyone wanted to test ride every day, but I sure did. That means that nearly every morning for two summers, I woke up, drove to work, and rode a 310-foot, ninety-three miles per hour roller coaster. I had the best view of the sun rising over Lake Erie and Sandusky Bay, and it sure put me in a good mood for the day. Nowadays I drink coffee to wake myself up, but back then, no caffeine was needed.

The ride remained my personal favorite, but there was one main thing that changed: the frequency of riding it. Riding it became a regular part of my job as if it was another day at the office. The anticipation of waiting in line was gone, and the thrill of riding it for the first time had faded years prior. For me, operating the ride, and even riding the ride, became routine, regular, and eventually, it felt redundant. I had ridden it at least 150 times, and most of those laps were by myself and as the sun was rising. This incredibly unique experience became something to check off my list as part of my job. Since it had to be done anyway, it was almost as if it was a chore. Then, during busy days in the summers that I worked at the park, the line would exceed 1.5–2 hours at peak times, sometimes longer. Guests would stand and wait for their one opportunity to experience what I was able to do every morning. The anticipation would build and some guests would become visibly nervous as they entered the load station. At that point, guests would frequently ask me, "Have you ridden this?" and I would reply, "Of course. I ride it every day."

It happened. The novelty and excitement of the ride had worn off.

Thankfully, I soon had a realization that allowed me to be excited about Millennium Force once again, similar to how I felt five years earlier. One morning, I was walking into work with one of my coworkers. It was before the park opened, and the atmosphere was calm and peaceful. As my coworker and I sleepily proceeded on our walk through the park, and when the ride's iconic lift hill came into view, my coworker stopped in his tracks and looked up, in the direction of the ride, and simply said, "Whoa." Out of a state of confusion, I asked what he was shocked by, and he simply gestured toward the ride and said quite matter of factly, "We get to push the buttons that make that thing go."

It was such a simple statement that in most circumstances would not have much impact. But that was the wake-up call I needed. I had allowed myself to become so accustomed to something that had given me such an exhilarating thrill until it became my job. If I maintained the mindset that allowed the excitement to fade, the actual ride experience would be less exciting for the guests riding. On the other hand, if I reminded myself that I "get to push the buttons that make the thing go," it would be the jolt of energy I needed to remember that this isn't regular and not everybody gets to do this like I do.

From that day forward, I allowed myself to retrieve the enthusiasm that I had for the ride, knowing that it was my favorite, and I demonstrated the desire to share that with guests who were experiencing the ride I was fortunate enough to experience on a daily basis, and especially with those who were riding for the first time. I accepted that perhaps for me it no longer carried the novelty that it once did because I had become so used to it, but when I recalled that enthusiasm for it from my time as a guest and from the first day that I had the privilege of "pushing the buttons to make the thing go," it would amp my enthusiasm. And when my enthusiasm for the experience was amped, it would elevate the experience for guests as well. The anticipation was stronger for guests about to board, and the screams were louder at the end when they were welcomed back.

Don't Let Excited Guests Bore You

I once checked into a resort hotel to visit a client in a highly popular tourist destination. This hotel is known for attracting affluent guests from all over the world and has a rich history that includes worldwide recognition, celebrities who played in the lobby lounge in their early days, along with countless television shows and movies that have been filmed at this location. The lobby is spacious and iconic, its views of the ocean are breathtaking, and to some, the spa is worth the trip alone. When I entered the lobby, even though I was visiting on business and not leisure, I could feel the excitement and the energy that the hotel naturally exudes. I proceeded to the front desk, waited several minutes in line, and was waived over by a front desk agent when I finally made it to the front of the line. "How may I assist you?" the agent asked. "I am here, and I'm checking in!" I announced proudly. Without smiling and while barely making eye contact as she pulled up her screen, she unenthusiastically said, "Identification and credit card, please."

I recognized that this agent was processing check-ins and checkouts all day, and given the length of the line, she had probably just checked in several guests in a row without a break. Her feet may have hurt and her eyes might have been getting strained from staring at her computer for too long. The process of checking guests was routine, typical, and in this case, redundant. She temporarily forgot where she was, along with the commitments people make to get there, and the excitement that guests have when they finally arrive. I even showed her that I was excited to be there, that for me this was not a regular component of my day or my life, but an event that I believed was heightened from my regular routine. But for her, another guest checking into this hotel was just another guest checking into this hotel.

Like my previous example of operating a world-class roller coaster, it was *perfectly fine* that checking in a guest was purely routine and a very ordinary component of her job. Any efficient operation thrives on routine and repetitive actions to ensure consistency in the delivery of the product or experience. However, the enthusiasm for your guests should be a compulsory component of the routine. It should be built into the job description of any guest-facing staff member beyond the standard of friendliness. When your enthusiasm is consistent, it may even feel redundant for you, and that is perfectly fine because your guests sense the novelty of what you have to offer, not the routine. By maintaining enthusiasm even when it feels redundant, your guests will never feel like they are "herded like cattle," as discussed in the previous chapter. Combine consistent enthusiasm with personalizing the guest experience, and every moment of truth that your guests experience will exceed their high expectations. Drop the enthusiasm, and the expectation of a unique experience will start to be challenged.

When Your Jokes Fly, You'll Hit the Jackpot

At "SlotZilla,"[14] a zipline attraction that soars over the Fremont Street Experience in Las Vegas, Nevada, the staff members effectively use their enthusiasm to improve the efficiency of the attraction. Every so often, they need a single rider to fill in what would otherwise be an empty spot on the zipline. When done in a timely manner, moving a single rider to the front of the line increases hourly throughput, allowing the operator to serve more guests per hour, and therefore makes the line slightly shorter each time. Urgency is key because holding up a dispatch to wait for a single rider has the opposite effect, and the efficiency of the operation declines. Since the queue is condensed and much of it includes waiting on the platform (which is at the top of a giant slot machine), they can reach a large audience at once to find a solo guest who is closest to the front of the line. Instead of making an announcement saying that they need to fill in the spot for efficiency and throughput purposes, they use a variety of creative spiels that are not only functional and important for the attraction's operations, but they are also entertaining. While waiting in line, you may hear, "Is there anyone out there who really doesn't like the people they're with and wants to ride before them? Now is your chance."

Also, since SlotZilla is in Las Vegas, they can afford to be a little edgier than most family entertainment attractions, which allows them to say things like, "If you came here with a ten but now the alcohol is wearing off and they've become a five, this is your chance to get away." This might not be the approach that would apply to all businesses, but tailoring these types of announcements to your guest can accomplish the functional needs of efficiency and throughput, while also giving them a more entertaining experience than they expected. When guests look back on their experience at SlotZilla, many will say that waiting in line was as much fun as the zipline itself. That type of guest response can only be achieved if those who are focused on delivering the experience make *themselves* as memorable as the product itself. It's efficient, it's entertaining, and most importantly, it's delivered with enthusiasm.

When you look at how the staff members at SlotZilla creatively enhance the experience and if you break down these quick remarks, you'll notice that these jokes most likely weren't made up on the spot. These little quips are embedded into their standard routine, as they know that they have a functional purpose of their job to operate the attraction efficiently and keep the line moving. Yet, they are well aware that waiting in line is not fun, and they have the ability to be the entertainment for their large audience—

and that's what Las Vegas is all about, right? This requires a combination of creativity, along with empowerment and encouragement from their leadership team. By implementing this into the culture, employees know from their first day on the job that this type of behavior is not just allowed, but rather, encouraged. It might sound intuitive that a zipline in Las Vegas that spits you out of a giant slot machine would automatically lend itself to a wackier vibe than most other types of experiences, but the enthusiasm that the employees exude is what defines how the guest perceives the nature of the attraction.

Because they aren't making up these jokes spontaneously, they are able to use the ones that test best with their audience, otherwise known as the guests waiting in line for the attraction. The jokes may not be scripted, nor are they required to say them, but if one operator comes up with a humorous way to ask for single riders that is effective, entertaining, and doesn't offend anybody, they can now work that into their routine. Their coworkers can now implement these remarks too, since they've been tested and found to exceed expectations, and they can come up with creative ways of their own. As long as the same joke isn't used repeatedly in front of the same group of guests (hence their need for variety, depending on the length of the queue), they can make these jokes all day, and while they may be saying it for the fiftieth time, the guest will be hearing it for the first time. The staff can allow it to become regular, routine, and even redundant, as long as they maintain their enthusiasm for it.

Burgers Are Just as Exciting

Enthusiasm isn't only reserved for the most iconic roller coasters, sought-after destination resorts, or a zipline jutting out of a giant slot machine. One of my favorite examples of when consistent enthusiasm works happened to me in a location smaller than three thousand square feet. Once, while visiting Orlando, I wandered into Beth's Burger Bar,[15] a fast-casual hamburger restaurant that was part of a small chain. I had never heard of it before, but I am always eager to try something new. Upon arrival, I knew that my level of commitment was low. If I didn't like what I saw, I easily would have been able to walk out without wasting anybody's time, especially my own. There were a few other options in the same complex as this burger place, including the more familiar staples and major franchises, so I knew I had nothing to lose. Nevertheless, right when I walked in, I was greeted enthusiastically by the staff member behind the counter, which was about ten to fifteen feet from the door. It was almost as if she was anticipating my arrival.

"Welcome!" she announced with a smile, showing that she was sincerely excited that I arrived. I had no choice but to match it, even though I had wandered in aimlessly, not expecting to be as enthusiastic as she was. "Hello!" I replied back. "It's my first time here!" And immediately her jaw dropped as she continued, "It's your first time?! Welcome! I'm so glad you stopped in!" I continued and told her that I had no idea what to order, and she immediately helped me understand the menu and asked me a few specific questions about what I liked and didn't like on my burgers. She ran through the different styles of patties, buns, and sauces, and when I determined which burger I wanted, she continued her excitement on what she recommended as her favorite sides. By the time my credit card was swiped, the transaction was substantially higher than it would have been if I had been greeted with a passive, "How may I help you?" And I wasn't mad about that. She allowed her enthusiasm to drive the conversation, and I was highly satisfied paying a few extra dollars for what she convincingly told me were her recommendations. She delivered a hyperpersonalized experience, identified specific characteristics about me that allowed her to make a recommendation, and seamlessly steered me in a direction where my transaction would be a little higher—while simultaneously making me feel very happy about the purchase I made and the amount I spent. Similar to the example in the last chapter with the scenario at the aquarium box office, the personalization was met with enthusiasm, and that simultaneously created a sale *and* created an enthusiastic guest.

I asked her how long the store had been open. She told me it had been about a year, and she had started shortly after the opening. Let that sink in as we run some quick numbers here. It was my first time in the restaurant, but it could have been her two hundredth if not even more than that. But even after her two hundredth day working at Beth's Burger Bar, she greeted me with the enthusiasm of someone on their first day; her energy overflowed contagiously, which amped up my experience and ultimately resulted in a higher sale. Compare this with the lack of enthusiasm I encountered while checking into the hotel. The experience that I had while ordering a takeout meal for less than $20 was more memorable than the arrival process at a destination resort where the rooms are typically between $300 and $400 per night. When you identify the enthusiasm that your guests have for your experience, and you retrieve the enthusiasm that you once had for it, you will take the guest experience to the next level, exceed their expectations, and ultimately open the door for higher revenue-generating opportunities.

Your culture of enthusiasm is a critical component of your guest service culture and embodying the Hospitality Mentality. At its core, your employees must *want* to show their enthusiasm for your guest experience, otherwise, they may not be a culture fit. Your service standard should not be "show your enthusiasm or else," but rather should naturally be shared based on the passion that you and your employees have for what you do. When passion is the key characteristic of each employee, the enthusiasm becomes natural, and even when it becomes routine and ordinary, it does not become redundant.

Notice that I am not suggesting that you should match your guests' level of enthusiasm; you should *go beyond* it. When discussing company culture and employee engagement, Joel Manby discusses how employee enthusiasm leads to guest satisfaction, along with lower turnover. As the former CEO of Herschend Family Entertainment and SeaWorld Parks and Resorts, and author of the book *Love Works*, Joel talks about the importance of training for guest engagement and measuring employee engagement along with it. Specifically, he said, "If your employees are engaged, your guest experience is going to be engaged . . . Your guest experience and the enthusiasm of it can never rise any higher than the enthusiasm of your own employees."[16] By focusing on these elements, Joel stated that guest satisfaction increased along with employee retention, thus supporting the company's financial goals: when guest satisfaction goes up, revenue goes up; when employee satisfaction goes up, hiring and training costs go down.

When the staff is more enthusiastic than their guests, the enthusiasm spills over into sharing the excitement, making the guest more enthused, leading to a higher likelihood of walking away satisfied. This is true whether it's an epic roller coaster, a destination resort, a zipline in a slot machine, or a hamburger. Okay, this all sounds great, but once leaders understand this, the next question revolves around *how do I stay enthused and keep frontline staff members enthused as well?* There are no strategies in this book that allow you to "set it and forget it," and move on to the next. Enthusiasm is only effective if it is sustained, expected, and consistent. That's where it gets tricky. People have bad days. They should be allowed to have bad days. People will also have good days where they might need some downtime, meaning that not every guest they interact with will see them at their peak energy level. There must be a balance of energy and enthusiasm, otherwise your tank will never stay full.

When fostering a culture of enthusiasm, those who embrace the Hospitality Mentality incorporate each of the following measures into their operation:

- Lead by example
- Observe and respond
- Recognize and reward
- Offer support
- Encourage personal enthusiasm
- Eliminate the script
- Share inspiring examples

Lead by example. It starts with you. Regardless of your role within your organization, if you wish to see ongoing enthusiasm from others, you must practice it and demonstrate it on a daily basis. If the goal is for your staff's enthusiasm to spill over to your guests, then the enthusiasm from leadership must spill over to all staff. Your job is to model the behavior that you expect from others. You cannot assume that frontline staff will be able to pick up on how to demonstrate enthusiasm when leadership will not do it first. If you want to see it done, show them how to do it best.

Observe and respond. When you spend most of your time back of house, you miss seeing your employees in action. Instead, focus on being where your guests are so you can lead by example, and more importantly, be where your employees are so that you can regularly observe behavior and jump in to give pointers as necessary. Giving feedback to employees is a critical part of ensuring consistency so that any incorrect behaviors can quickly be remedied and exemplary behavior can grow upon itself.

Recognize and reward. What gets recognized gets repeated. If your rock stars aren't recognized for being rock stars, they will quickly fade into the background. Share with your staff your own excitement for their enthusiasm, and make sure they know why it was such a great job. If you have a recognition program that rewards these types of moments, make it your job to reward your staff whenever possible. Rewards and incentives can be monetary, but they don't need to be. Thanking the team member with genuine sincerity gives a boost of confidence that will lead to the next enthusiastic moment.

Offer support. If an employee is having a bad day or a frustrating moment, and you're able to cover for them or have them relieved, give them that break to recharge. Even fifteen minutes can be enough for someone to clear their head and get back in the game, but if it's bigger than that, maybe they need to head home for the day. Sending an employee home for not demonstrating enthusiasm shouldn't be avoided if it's necessary, and it also shouldn't be seen as punishment; they aren't benefiting the guest, their team, and most importantly, themselves by not being able to be fully present. Be there to support your staff members when they need your support.

Encourage personal enthusiasm. Just like the team at Slot-Zilla crafted their own jokes and worked them into their routine, allowing your team to create their own way of communicating with guests helps them deliver a hyperpersonalized experience, allowing staff to share their enthusiasm, and making the required elements of the experience feel remarkable. Let them come up with their own ways to create a unique experience, meaning it might be different from one staff member to the next. This adds value to the guest experience because tying in the personal touch shows that the experience should not be robotic or scripted. That leads to the next point . . .

Eliminate the script. Requiring a script to be read verbatim is the best way to kill enthusiasm. If there are specific words or phrases that *must* be communicated verbatim, indicate what verbiage cannot be altered, and leave the rest open for your staff to find their own way of phrasing what needs to be phrased. Give them guidelines and point them in the direction of what needs to be said, asked, communicated, or offered, and allow each employee to come up with their own enthusiastic way to deliver it. Reading a dry script word for word is worse than redundant—it's boring. Think of a flight attendant delivering safety instructions. Who do you pay attention to more, flight attendants who read the exact words that passengers need to hear or the ones who have fun with it while getting across all the required key messages?

Share inspiring examples. Don't assume that your staff knows exactly how to maintain energy and create enthusiastic moments for guests. Give them specific examples of how they can share their enthusiasm based on what you've done, what you've seen, or what you would like to see. Share these in preshift meetings, through internal communication channels, and during impromptu conversations so that they can see into your mind. Make sure to stress that it's not about what they *have* to do, it's about what they *get* to do.

The concept of enthusiasm may come across as abstract, particularly because what might be considered enthusiastic behavior for one person might be different for someone else. It's more difficult to measure than other employee standards, such as arriving to work on time, being in proper uniform, and meeting operational goals; however, it can be influenced, observed, and recognized. By now, you know that encouraging enthusiasm from a leadership viewpoint is more than telling your employees to smile and be upbeat, which can often backfire particularly during times of high stress. Part of showing enthusiasm includes going back to the basics discussed in chapter 1 and highlighting key standards such as projecting a friendly attitude, making eye contact, and greeting the guest first. It doesn't force a smile on anyone's face, but rather sets the stage for what guests expect along with what is expected from them. Then, layering in the elements from this chapter, allow for enthusiasm to come across much more naturally and frequently.

Chapter 6 Strategy Statement:

We are even more enthusiastic than our guests, and we do not let the novelty factor wear off or become redundant.

Chapter 7:
Anticipate Guests' Needs

———— 🍍 ————

The year was 2010. Anthony and Angie had just landed in Tokyo after a long flight from Montreal. After taking the train to Shinjuku Station, one of the busiest stations in the city, they were both overwhelmed and exhausted. Without proficiency in speaking Japanese, combined with a lack of wayfinding in the streets, finding their hotel could have easily been a miserable experience. Smartphones had yet to reach widespread adoption, so the conveniences we have today to solve this type of problem were not available. They had to get around the old-fashioned way. Being unfamiliar with the area and not even knowing where to begin, this was destined to be a horrible start to their trip.

Fortunately, they had printed the English instructions provided to them by their hotel geared toward travelers beginning at Shinjuku, which included a map of the immediate area. Upon opening the instructions, their mood changed entirely. Anthony and Angie both felt that the instructions were tailored just for them, and when they exited the station and reviewed the map, the first instruction said, "Look up." This very specific instruction allowed them to locate the first landmark, or the clue on this treasure hunt that the hotel wanted them to solve. The landmark was a sign for KFC, a familiar brand, which helped them ensure that the next clue would be followed exactly as directed. "Take 20 steps in the direction of the KFC sign." This level of clarity eliminated all the stress of finding the hotel. According to Anthony, "It was linear, it was clear, and it was very efficient."

Once they walked into the hotel, the staff intuitively knew who they were. Anthony joked that the hotel employees were on the lookout for a Canadian couple, which allowed them to deliver a hyperpersonalized experience. "They welcomed me by name, and the whole thing from start to finish, all the way until we left, was like that." I asked Anthony why this was such a monumental moment, and he said, "I felt that they thought about me when they wrote that message. I felt like I was the center of the experience. I don't know if they knew that I would be coming off of a fifteen-hour flight. I don't know if they knew that I don't read or speak Japanese. I don't know if they know that I don't know that there are no street signs. It felt like they said, 'We know this guy.'"

Anthony said that the anticipation of his needs continued throughout his stay. Upon checking into their room, housekeeping had already turned the room down and closed the drapes because they understood that even though it was 2:00 p.m., they would probably be exhausted and would want to sleep. For the remainder of the stay, turndown service was only done in the evening, as expected, meaning that there was intentional and thoughtful effort to prepare the room in such a way for the guests' arrival. Not every guest would need the same treatment because not every guest would be arriving in the same state. Another guest or couple traveling domestically within Japan probably would not need for the room to be turned down in the same way when they check in; they might want to drop their luggage and hit the town.

Guests should not have to ask for this type of service or these types of amenities. By implementing chapter 6's tactics of personalizing the experience, the staff at the hotel not only centered their service around Anthony and Angie but extended it further into breaking down what their basic needs would be. They wouldn't have expected to have such clear instructions that directed them from the train station to the hotel, nor would they have expected the room to be in nighttime mode in the middle of the afternoon. Therefore, this *anticipation of their needs* exceeded their expectations, which led Anthony to share this story with me more than a decade later.

If we turn this situation around, what if the hotel had provided a consistent, cookie-cutter experience to Anthony and Angie that was exactly the same as every other guest, regardless of circumstance? A ubiquitous approach would have been to provide instructions in Japanese, possibly with translations in many other languages in the same document, with instructions that included every possible origin with multiple modes of transportation. This would require the guest to locate what applied to them and sift through the text to find their native language. Then, after likely getting lost and asking a stranger for help (hopefully they could communicate with each other), they would show up even more exhausted than they were to begin with. While checking in, the room might not even be available yet, as 2:00 p.m. is earlier than a standard guarantee at most hotels. After storing their luggage and sitting in the lobby, feeling like zombies (and probably looking like zombies too), they would later proceed to their room and quickly need to close the drapes to avoid being blasted with sunlight, followed by an immediate crash.

Treating all guests the same would have been the easy solution, and the flow of the arrival process would have met exactly what the hotel was looking for. Also, because it wouldn't have been the hotel's fault that Anthony and Angie would have gotten lost or that they were exhausted, there would be nothing to complain about. Without anticipating their needs, the hotel could still have done everything right. But instead of just being right, the hotel staff decided to be *remarkable*. This could only be done by identifying who the guest was and what circumstances they were bringing with them into the hotel, and using the resources that they had to make the experience even better than what the guest expected. This story is a perfect example of anticipating guests' needs.

Anticipating guests' needs boils down to these four factors:

1. Combine your proficiency with awareness of the guest in front of you
2. Recognize when guests don't know what they don't know
3. Answer the questions that your guests didn't know they had
4. Never make assumptions

Combine Your Proficiency with Awareness of the Guest in Front of You

Your training and expertise are put to the test when you align your knowledge of the facility with what the guest might need or what information will benefit them. In some ways, it's simply using your own common sense to make a recommendation to a guest that goes beyond what they expected or would have asked for themselves.

Recognize When Guests Don't Know What They Don't Know

Your guests may not be familiar with your environment. They might not know what to do upon arrival, and they may not even realize how little they know. And that's okay. When guests give you the signal that they aren't quite sure what's going on, that's when it's time to intervene.

Answer the Questions that Your Guests Didn't Know They Had

If guests don't know what they don't know, then they might not ask questions that will benefit them or their experience. This can even lead to a negative perception of the experience that could have been avoided if the guest had more information. By recognizing when guests *aren't* speaking up when perhaps they should, your anticipation of needs can enhance their experience.

Never Make Assumptions

Anticipating does not mean assuming. On occasion, these are even polar opposites. You never want to assume that the guest knows what they're doing, but you don't want to assume that they don't know either or you risk offending them. By actively offering assistance from an anticipatory standpoint rather than an assumptive one, the guest will sense your hospitality, and not see it as an intrusion.

There is a word in Japanese that defines Anthony and Angie's experience in Tokyo: *omotenashi*. As a rough translation, *omotenashi* means "hospitality" in Japanese; however, the definition extends far beyond just that word. It's an entire philosophy, and according to hospitality training firm Otolo, this philosophy changed hospitality entirely.[17] *Omotenashi* originated from tea ceremonies, and the philosophy consists of three interconnected and equally important parts: empathy, authenticity, and anticipation.

When it comes to empathy, this consists of having respect and consideration for the guest, along with a deep understanding of the guest's expectations and desires. Authenticity dictates that staff should express genuine appreciation for the guest and make the guest feel as valued as possible. Both of these components are woven through the chapters of this book.

The third leg of *omotenashi* is anticipation. Otolo describes anticipation, as it relates to *omotenashi*, as follows:

> *Attention to detail is key with this philosophy; the customer's every need is anticipated and a great effort is exerted in order to meet these needs. Every member of staff must have a desire to understand the customer and believe that there is no task that is too difficult or menial. Even non-customer-facing employees must have this value deeply rooted in them in order to ensure that the customer has the best experience possible.*

Not only are the needs anticipated, but the effort that is exerted demonstrates (a) that you know your guest and the experience you intend to deliver them, and (b) you have the resources, tools, infrastructure, and empowerment to get it done, even if it breaks the mold of your standard operation. This is further proven by stressing that no task is too difficult or menial, meaning that regardless of what the guest needs or desires, you are equipped and ready to make it happen, whether the guest directly asked for it or not—or even if they knew to ask for it or not. The culture that you build must have unanimous buy-in from each and every team member, otherwise, your hospitality engine will not be able to run at full energy. Lastly, your culture of hospitality does not end at the barriers to your front of house, but every individual within the organization is living and breathing your service standard and the importance of anticipating guests' needs.

Examples of *omotenashi* in Japanese hospitality include the following:

- A toothpick nicely wedged between the indentation of a pair of wooden chopsticks
- Umbrella and bag holders placed within hand's reach at a Japanese ATM
- Taxi drivers with white gloves, lace on the seats, and taxi doors that open automatically by the driver via a special lever inside the cab[18]
- Baskets for guests' bags or coats beside tables in restaurants and bars
- Water and a hot towel provided for guests as they are seated in a restaurant

Omotenashi encompasses so many elements of the Hospitality Mentality, but anticipating guests' needs is arguably the closest comparison. Are you answering questions that guests never knew they had and designing your experience around eliminating potential frustrations?

Let the Experts Help the Novices

Who is the expert at your operation? Who's the expert on your guest experience? Your rules, procedures, and policies? Who has the expertise that will ensure the best possible experience? Is it you or your guests?

It's relatively easy to allow guests to go through their experience without handholding or intervention, especially when they look like they know what they're doing. Perhaps they have been before and can reference a previous experience, perhaps they have conducted thorough research, or perhaps they give off no indication that they aren't the expert. In some cases, it may be true. Hopefully, your best guests are not only your most loyal, but they are the experts who are even training less proficient guests to share the knowledge through their guidance and wisdom.

On the other hand, many guests have no idea what they're doing. This will often result in a subpar experience because they expected more and didn't experience all that they were aware of, or it might even result in satisfaction due to blissful naivety. In either case, there exists an opportunity to jump in and use your knowledge and your expertise to answer questions that guests might not think to ask. Anticipating guests' needs is when expertise and proficiency are combined with awareness, and in some cases plain common sense. It requires on-the-spot foresight that sometimes will go beyond functional job duties. It requires more than showing up for work; it requires being present with every guest with whom you interact. If you or your staff are simply going through the motions and checking boxes to cover the functional points of each guest interaction, it will only meet expectations . . . and sometimes may not even do that. You may notice the common thread from personalizing the experience, maintaining enthusiasm, and now anticipating guests' needs: they all require doing just a *little bit more* than what the guest expects but doing it consistently.

When you anticipate guests' needs, it creates an opportunity for you to prove that you are the experts in your business and that you are truly committed to ensuring that all of your guests have a positive experience. Anticipating guests' needs is when you recognize that oftentimes your guests *don't know what they don't know*. It is your responsibility to determine what the guest may need or want that they don't know how to ask for. And in some cases, a guest may ask a question without knowing that perhaps the question they are asking is not relevant to the actual answer that they need. When you can look a little further down the line, you can exceed guests' expectations by offering more information or providing a higher service than they requested, thus anticipating your guests' needs.

Using Proficiency to Ask Questions that Guests Wouldn't Think to Ask

Guests may need information that they may not think to ask for. When I worked in the Guest Communications team at Universal Orlando (which at the time handled the Guest Services call center), I once answered a call from a guest who had a very simple question: "What is the height requirement for Dudley Do-Right's Ripsaw Falls?" Despite the long name, the answer was short, simple, and straightforward. And with my proficiency in the resort and all its attractions, I knew off the top of my head that the answer was a minimum of 44 inches.[19] However, instead of answering his question immediately, I responded with another question: When are you visiting? The guest told me he was coming in about a month and asked why I wanted to know. The reason I asked was that he made this call at some point in the winter, which is a time that the water rides are occasionally closed for seasonal maintenance for a couple of weeks, due to the lower temperatures in Orlando. Thankfully, he was planning a visit after the ride was scheduled to reopen, and I provided him with the information requested; however, if he was calling from the car on the way to the park, I had the knowledge and ability to anticipate something that he would not have otherwise have known to ask.

Let's say that was the case. Let's say the guest called and asked a simple question, and I gave him a simple answer. He is in the car with his child who is 45 inches tall, just over the height requirement, and he excitedly tells the child that they will be able to ride. They drive from home, spend a considerable amount of money to park their car, walk from the parking garage to the ticket booth (this might take twenty to twenty-five minutes), buy tickets, get into the park, and proceed all the way to the back of the park where the ride is located. They are greeted less than hospitably by a fence plastered with signs saying something to the effect of "Ride closed for seasonal maintenance." The child would be upset, likely inconsolable, and the man would have said, "Why didn't Josh tell me this when I called about the height requirement?" Continuing the hypothetical scenario, let's say the man remembered my name and complained to Guest Services, and ultimately it got back to me. If I was asked why I hadn't told him that the ride was closed, I would have said, "Well, he didn't ask me if the ride was open. He just wanted to know how tall you had to be to ride." Sure, but now what? That statement would not have excused me from failing to anticipate the one thing the man needed to know—the ride is not open—making the question about the height requirement irrelevant. Fortunately, I did ask him, and even more fortunately, he planned to visit once the scheduled maintenance was expected to be complete.

Your guests will not always know what they don't know because they are not the experts at your operation. They are not as familiar with rules, procedures, policies, layout, scheduled events, and scheduled maintenance as you and your staff are. Guests may try to carry someone in a stroller or wheelchair up a flight of stairs because they didn't know that there was a ramp on the other side of the building. Guests might smoke in a children's area because they didn't know that there is a designated smoking area. Guests may arrive fifteen minutes before you close because they didn't check your operating hours before they visited. By anticipating what guests need in that moment, you show that you are demonstrating proficiency in your operation and your organization and that you are constantly on the lookout for these types of interactions that will ultimately provide an experience that exceeds their expectations.

How Do You Anticipate Guests' Needs? Treat Them Like They're Aliens.

Several years ago, I was chatting with my friend Andrea, who was in the process of opening a brewery and was hired to manage the taproom. This would include all front-of-house operations, including bartenders, servers, and the hospitality element of the business. Andrea was building her orientation and training program, so naturally, I asked her about her hospitality philosophy and what would go into her training.

"My philosophy can be summed up like this: treat your guests like aliens visiting from another planet." She said this quite matter-of-factly, and I knew she wasn't joking, but I had no idea what she meant. "Treat them like aliens?" I asked. I had to learn more.

"Treat them like aliens because, in many ways, they are. They are coming into an environment that is completely unfamiliar, almost like an entirely different planet. They don't know our customs, they don't know our pricing or payment processes, we don't always speak the same language with the specific verbiage that we use, and they don't have nearly the knowledge and awareness that we have of what goes on within these walls. This is our domain, and they may as well be visiting from another planet. We need to make sure they have the best experience possible while on our planet, and it's up to us to give them everything they need."

Now this made perfect sense. While some of her explanation was certainly more figurative than literal, she made so many good points. A first-time visitor doesn't even know where the bathroom is, so how should they be expected to know everything else about your business?

When you treat your guests like aliens visiting from another planet, you anticipate their needs and you never make assumptions that they know how your operation works, what your rules and policies are, or even how to spend more money. Sure, some guests are better informed than others, especially those who visit regularly, but you cannot assume that every guest has the same knowledge that you have. If you ask probing questions, such as whether they have visited before or whether they know what they'd like to buy, you can sift out the first-timers from the veterans and customize the way you serve them based on what will be best for them. The Hospitality Mentality is not a one-size-fits-all approach.

Oh—and what happens when your aliens get upset? They say, "*Take me to your leader.*" When that happens, it's time to jump into complaint resolution mode, which will be covered in extensive detail in chapter 10.

Calculated Anticipation vs. Making Assumptions

In Anthony and Angie's example, the staff at the hotel in Tokyo made a decision to alter the guest experience based on anticipating what the guest might need. In some ways, this was a gamble. What if they weren't tired when they checked in? Perhaps they would have arrived at their room, full of energy, and wondered why housekeeping decided to tone it down for their visit. What if they had visited Tokyo multiple times, were fluent in Japanese, and knew exactly where the hotel was located in relation to the train station?

Had this been the case, one could argue that the hotel staff made an assumption that a couple flying from Montreal to Tokyo would be unable to locate the hotel and would need to go straight to bed when they arrived. If executed poorly, it would have led to a negative experience, with the thought that the staff made an assumption of what they would need. Instead, the staff acted based on what they anticipated the guest *might* need when they arrived and acted accordingly. They made a calculated anticipation. If Anthony and Angie didn't need the directions, they would have discarded them. If they weren't jetlagged when they checked in, they would have opened the drapes.

It is important to note the distinction between anticipating guests' needs and assuming guests' needs. Assumptions occur with a lack of foresight, not when there is too much. Assuming that a guest will want or need something can become an awkward friction point that leads to a negative experience. By understanding who your guest is as you strive to deliver a hyperpersonalized experience, the information that you gain allows you to make more calculated anticipations and reduces the risk of making an assumption.

As we know by now, calculated anticipations are the result of combining the proficiency of your operation with the awareness of the individual needs of the guest. When a restaurant patron orders steak, replace their standard knife with a steak knife. When it starts to rain by the pool, put up the umbrellas over the lounge chairs for guests who have left items there. When passengers deplane after a long flight, tell them whether they need to go left or right to get to baggage claim. When a guest in a theme park walks into a line for an attraction wearing a loose article that is sure to fall off, let them know where they can store it while they ride. At a highly attended convention with multiple transportation options to nearby hotels, color-code the routes on the signage so attendees can quickly find their ride. Your goal should be to eliminate the guesswork that your guests will need to do and minimize the likelihood that their experience will be negatively impacted. When guests recognize these gestures, they often notice the heightened sense of service that is being delivered.

Where Are We at So Far?

With proper training and ongoing coaching, each of these three strategies can be implemented into your standard operating procedures (SOPs):

1. Deliver a hyperpersonalized experience
2. Be more enthusiastic than your guest
3. Anticipate guests' needs

Once these strategies are woven into your SOP, new hires can be immersed into the culture upon beginning their employment. When staff members are informed from day one that exceeding expectations is part of their job duties, it becomes much more natural for them to immediately start personalizing the experience with guests, showing their enthusiasm (even if it feels redundant), and anticipating guests' needs. By building it into your service standard and culture, it flows from your staff seamlessly. And with their peers demonstrating the example, new employees see that the bar is set high, and they will either naturally gravitate toward the elevated standard, or they will recognize quickly that it is not for them. Both options are good for all parties, and when the standard is emphasized during recruitment and interviewing, then the latter scenario should happen less frequently.

If these three strategies can be applied across the board, you will elevate your standard, knowing that the human element of your operation is going to be the factor that makes or breaks the guest experience. Your service standard is the differentiator between you and your competitors, whether they be direct or indirect or fall into the never-ending "everything else" category. But we can push the envelope even further. If these three methods go a mile wide and an inch deep, what happens when we go an inch wide and a mile deep? What can you do that you cannot do with every guest every time, but when you do it, its impact is so lasting that the likelihood of loyalty is exponential compared with a standard satisfactory experience? What will people immediately share on social media and cause them to immediately start planning their next visit? There are multiple things that you can do that will supply your guests with talking points to amplify their audience via word of mouth, both within their personal circles and online through review websites. To help define what those may be, move on to the next chapter to look at the final step of exceeding your guests' expectations.

Chapter 7 Strategy Statement:

We anticipate our guests' needs by answering questions they did not know they had, combining our proficiency of the business with awareness of each guest's unique circumstance.

Chapter 8:
Make an Impact with "Wow" Moments

———— 🍍 ————

"Welcome back, Mr. Liebman."

The front desk agent looked up at me from his monitor, smiled, made direct eye contact, and continued. "We see that you've arrived early, and I'm pleased to tell you that your room is ready. Your reservation states that you booked a standard room, although we have a little surprise for you."

The agent briefly broke eye contact to signal a slight head nod to a coworker on the other side of the lobby, then returned his attention to me and smiled again. "Antonio will be taking you from here. I hope you enjoy your stay." Right then, my luggage was swept away on a bell cart, and a staff member who introduced himself as Antonio greeted me within three seconds. "Mr. Liebman, if you are ready, follow me."

This was off to a good start, but I knew the drill by this point. Antonio would have checked all the boxes with a quick welcome back, asked me how long it's been since my last visit, and tell me whether there were any renovations or additional dining options that have opened between then and now. Bonus points if he pointed out the emergency exits and offered to fill my ice bucket.

A warm welcome and friendly service are purely table stakes when you arrive at any Ritz-Carlton property. Its superior standard creates an expectation so high that it's a challenge to go even higher.

But it's a fun challenge, and Antonio was up for it. "What brings you into town?" he asked in the elevator. While many guest service ambassadors would enjoy calm silence while leading a guest to their room, Antonio recognized an opportunity to build rapport. During the conversation, Antonio ascertained the reason for the visit, where I was coming in from, and what I planned to do during my stay. "Beach, pool, bar . . . rinse and repeat." Antonio smiled and approved of the itinerary.

"Right this way, Mr. Liebman." Antonio led me down a long, pristine hallway, pushing the bell cart as I followed behind him. His conversation continued as we discussed recent sporting events and local events, and he assured me that the weather during my visit was expected to be phenomenal—almost as if he had arranged it that way.

At the end of the hallway, Antonio stopped and turned back around. "Mr. Liebman, thank you again for staying with us and for trusting us to make memories for you this week. We're thrilled that you've come back to visit, and thank you for being a Platinum member with Marriott Rewards.[20] We've taken the liberty of switching your reservation to a different room type, but I don't think you'll mind."

Antonio opened the door to an 800-square-foot oceanfront suite, more than double the size of the room I had expected. It had a living area, dining room, two bathrooms, a massive wraparound porch, and a perfect view of the ocean. Antonio led the luggage cart into the room, unloaded my suitcase onto a luggage rack, and gave a full orientation of the room, which naturally took several minutes due to the size and the number of amenities. I was asked about dining and spa reservations and informed of how to secure my lounge chairs at the beach and pool. At the end of the tour, Antonio introduced himself again, thanked me by name, and advised me what to do if I needed anything at all, at any time. Lastly, he pointed out the emergency exit procedures, offered to fill the ice bucket, and extended a genuine parting remark, hoping I enjoyed my visit.

There was only one word that came to mind when Antonio left the room. And that word was "wow." It wasn't just that I had gotten a free upgrade, but it was the way in which it was delivered. It was so carefully crafted in a way that not only would I be satisfied with my alternate accommodations, but the front desk agent and Antonio had strategically created a hyperpersonalized experience that maintained enthusiasm and anticipated my needs. The combination of the three led to an incredible "wow" moment that was a surefire way to imprint a lasting memory that wouldn't fade easily. They couldn't do this for every guest every day, and they knew that. This was a moment where the staff identified an opportunity to extend the experience far beyond the expectation and justified it as loyalty appreciation, which was brought up to me multiple times during the check-in and arrival process. And of course, that room type had to be available for the duration of my stay.

In this fourth method of exceeding expectations, we combine the principles of the previous three chapters and we take it in a direction where we know we can't do it for everyone. And that's okay. By following the formula of a "wow" moment, you can uncover so many opportunities for more and more guests to feel the impact of your superior hospitality, where they have an experience that is so far beyond what they expected, the likelihood of loyalty surges.

The formula for a "wow" moment can be defined as follows:

1. It surprises and delights.
2. It goes beyond the employee's job duties.
3. It does not detract from any other guest's experience.
4. It costs little or nothing to implement.

It Surprises and Delights

Exceeding expectations is exactly that: going above and beyond what a guest expects will happen during their experience. This is why "wow" moments often combine one, two, or all three of the previous chapters so that these moments are hyperpersonalized, delivered with enthusiasm, and anticipatory of guests' needs. They both surprise and delight guests in a way that puts a smile on their faces.

It Goes Beyond the Employee's Job Duties

Because "wow" moments cannot be delivered to every guest on every occasion, they are generally considered to be an act that goes beyond what is in the staff training manual. However, staff members must be encouraged and empowered to "wow" guests at every opportunity, while following the framework presented here.

It Does Not Detract from Any Other Guest's Experience

What if that suite had been occupied? If Antonio had walked into the room, kicked out the guests that were in there, and said, "Sorry, Josh is here. He's loyal to us and you're not," that would still make me say "Wow," but not for the right reasons, let alone how awkward that would have been. Instead, because that specific guestroom was available, the staff connected the dots and determined that they could give me that room as a free upgrade without anyone being upset about it.

It Costs Little or Nothing to Implement

"Wow" moments do not have to give away the farm. In fact, even in this example of the free room upgrade where the rate difference may have been several hundred dollars, the actual cost of the upgrade was a slight increase in labor and utilities. It was seen to be a worthy expense in the interest of creating an even more memorable experience for a guest.

From 2007 to 2008, Walt Disney World in Orlando and Disneyland in Anaheim both ran a campaign called the "Year of a Million Dreams" (yes, they extended it to two years and kept the same name, but that's not the important part). As you may recall, this was a time when the economy was taking a turn for the worst, and a trip to a Disney resort was likely one of the first things to get cut from a family's budget. Even though attendance was down, Disney saw this as an opportunity to provide more intimate experiences to guests. For context, providing a personalized, intimate experience is easier when you serve a small number of people at a time; entertaining north of thirty thousand paying visitors on a slow day makes it much more difficult. As a result, a team was formed called the "Dream Squad," whose mission was simple, yet effective, and incredibly important: make dreams come true, which Disney stayed on-brand with by referring to them as "Magical Moments."

These moments ranged on a very wide spectrum. Dream Squad Cast Members had the ability to approach guests at their discretion or were assigned to guests who were literally in the right place at the right time. Certain moments included FastPasses that allowed for expedited queueing to an attraction or immediate access via a personal escort through the VIP entrance. It could be popcorn, ice cream, a mouse ears hat, or other small things that the guest did not expect and did not pay for, and the moments retained a high value because they could not be given to every single guest. The more Magical Moments that could be delivered, the more guests would travel home and share the experience with others, building advocacy in the brand at a time when it was so badly needed.

The most amazing moment, however, happened once a day, and it was a massive responsibility for the Dream Squad because the impact that it provided was more memorable than popcorn or ice cream, or even a private meet and greet with the boss himself, Mickey Mouse. The moment that I'm referencing is when one family was chosen every day (I repeat: *Every. Single. Day.*), and was told that they would be spending the night *inside* Cinderella Castle.[21] The accommodation, known as the Dream Suite, was actually designed for Walt himself, though he was never fortunate enough to see the project come to fruition. At Disneyland in Anaheim, due to the size of the castle being much smaller than the one in Orlando, the Dream Suite was just as impressively located in an area tucked away, above a building in the New Orleans Square section of the park.

There is certainly a cost factor to this. Staffing the Dream Squad alone was a large labor operation. Then, the cost of each of the items they would give away, and of course, the cost of operating the Dream Suite on both coasts was quite expensive. You could not book it and could not pay for it, meaning it was like they were running a free hotel. There were maintenance costs, housekeeping costs, and additional labor costs that included a twenty-four-hour concierge that was at their service if they needed or wanted anything. However, think about the return on investment by bringing back up the three actions of loyal guests: they return, they spread the word, and they defend. Do you think these guests are going to return at some point? Sure. Granted, they probably won't have that same experience again, nor would they expect that, and this moment solidified a memory in their life that *cannot* be erased. Think of the children in those families—when they grow up, they are probably going to take their children to the place where they spent the night in a castle. Also, will they keep that experience discreet? Nope. They will see to it that every human with whom they come in contact for the foreseeable future will know that *they* were the family that was chosen to stay in the Dream Suite that day. And while I cannot speak for those guests directly, it is probably safe to say that if anyone says one bad word about the parks or the company, they are probably pretty quick to share their side of the argument. This was a long-game investment.

I present this example first because it is likely the pinnacle of the "wow" moment. There is not much in the area of hospitality, attractions, and tourism that can surpass the impact of this initiative (if you said "challenge accepted" after reading that sentence, I applaud you, and I am eager to see your response). Before moving on, though, I want to work backward and deconstruct this. Disney implemented this initiative knowing that attendance was declining due to the economy, meaning that guests who were making the trek truly needed to be recognized (remember, families who opted not to visit Disney parks due to financial constraints were doing an alternative that falls into the "everything else" category: doing nothing and saving money). However, the Dream Squad and its initiatives were not the company's first rodeo. Disney has been recognized for decades as being a leader and a pioneer in guest experience, and while the concept of "Magical Moments" was not created with this initiative, it was taken to a new level. More importantly, the correct order was taken. Even though the Dream Squad could not interact with every guest, the service standard for *all* Cast Members incorporated the three main elements of exceeding guests' expectations: personalizing the experience, maintaining enthusiasm, and anticipating guests' needs. Guests who were lucky enough to be approached by the Dream Squad in any capacity, from receiving popcorn to a night in the castle, were not the only guests who were benefiting from the service culture. The service standard still dictated that every guest would have a greater experience than they expected, and through the other three methods discussed in the previous three chapters, Cast Members were able to go above and beyond for every guest with whom they interacted. And as we back up even further, before the three core elements of exceeding expectations were implemented, the focus on meeting expectations was just as high, every single second of the day at every location throughout their properties. Custodial and maintenance crews worked around the clock; even paint crews were constantly keeping the colors fresh and inviting, knowing how cleanliness and maintenance factor so highly into immersing the guest into the environment they were promising. Each of the core eight expectations from chapter 3 needed to be addressed before they could start dishing out Magical Moments.

I imagine that you might now be saying something along the lines of "I don't have an iconic castle with a Dream Suite. How can I still surprise and delight my guests through 'wow' moments that go far beyond their expectations?" Fortunately, just like the other three strategies discussed, this method also can be applied to a full spectrum of situations. Some of these moments are larger than others. While the larger moments will have a longer-lasting impact on your guests, small moments can still magnify the gap between expectation and reality, with reality reigning supreme.

"Wow" Moments Should Be Delivered from the Frontline in a Spontaneous Manner

Let's take another page out of Ritz-Carlton's book, and this time from a different location. I arrived alone, as I was traveling for work, and knew that I wouldn't have much free time to do any sightseeing in the area or enjoy many of the amenities at the hotel. While checking in, the front desk agent went through all of the major functional points of the check-in process and did well to personalize the experience by using my name, engaging in a brief conversation, and showing enthusiasm that I was visiting the hotel. Near the end of the check-in process, when I expected to be handed a key packet and directed to the elevators, the agent looked at his screen behind the desk, leaned back slightly, and let out a slight, "Hmmph." I wasn't quite sure where this was going.

"Mr. Liebman," he said. "I see that you are here for one night. We're actually at very low occupancy this evening as we're in a slower time of the year for business. I noticed that you did not book any spa treatments. You are welcome to if you would like; however, if you wanted to simply enjoy the spa facility, I'm going to provide a separate key in your key packet if you want to use the spa. Normally this is reserved for guests who have spa treatments, but due to our low occupancy tonight, and more importantly, due to your loyalty to Marriott and Ritz-Carlton, I'm going to provide it to you at no cost. We have a beautiful spa facility, complete with a variety of heated and chilled pools, whirlpools, a sauna, and a steam room. You certainly don't have to use it if you don't want to, but you've got it if you want it."

I was amazed at this level of service. It was so quick and seemingly spontaneous, and it was as seamless as the rest of the check-in process itself. It did not require a manager's intervention for approval, yet the difference between my expectation and the reality was significant. If you break this down, this has many of the same elements as what Dream Squad Cast Members would do for Disney park guests. These elements included the following:

- It was a service I did not request.
- It was a service I did not expect.
- I was not expected to pay extra for this service.
- The employee who gave it to me was empowered to do so without going through levels of permission.
- This could not be done for every guest.
- I was surprised.
- I was delighted.
- The overall cost was minimal.
- He aligned it with a reason, which would manage my expectation in the future.

While the cost of the Dream Suite may have been a significant daily operational expense, what was the cost of giving me access to the spa? There were a few towels to launder, a bottle of water that I drank, and I suppose a small utility cost of the water in the spa that would have most likely been spent anyway. Furthermore, he specifically acknowledged that occupancy was low, which arguably meant that all of the maintenance and operating costs that were fixed expenses that were going into the spa would have been wasted if guests weren't enjoying it. There was no additional labor cost than what was already allocated since the treatment was not included in his offer, which also meant that it wasn't displacing any potential revenue that would have otherwise been gained. When it came down to it, the arguments for giving me access to the spa, even though I didn't ask for them, significantly outweighed the arguments for not giving me access, which I never would have noticed anyway. This moment surprised me, and I was delighted that it was offered and fulfilled so seamlessly. Wow!

Crafting "Wow" Moments

At this point, you have the concept and the framework, and now it's time to consider how you can implement "wow" moments into your service culture so that they are delivered on a regular basis, leading to more and more guests naturally walking into a delightfully surprising experience. Since "wow" moments are highly personal, they cannot be easily replicated from other businesses, but instead formed in-house, using the resources at your disposal.

When considering how to turn the concept into reality, you should seek to answer the following two questions:

1. What's the most you can imagine doing for your guests?
2. What's your mic-drop moment?

To answer the first question, let's look at the leader in rental homes, Airbnb. Founded in 2008, Airbnb has proven itself in the hospitality industry for short-term vacation rentals, mid-term remote working, and even business travel. In order to do this, founders Brian Chesky, Joe Gebbia, and Nathan Blecharczyk needed to look at the experience that their hosts were providing and strive to push the envelope beyond what their competitors were doing.[22] While many businesses, particularly those in hospitality, seek to deliver a five-star experience, the Airbnb team looked at five-stars as the starting line, not the finish line. As they brainstormed what six-, seven-, and eight-star experiences at Airbnb would look like, they extended their creative minds far beyond the realm of feasibility. When they finally defined what an eleven-star experience could look like, it involved showing up at the airport where Elon Musk looks at you and says, "We're going to space."

The eleven-star experience wasn't intended to be realistic (although Musk has been to space since then, so you never know). As they pulled back and reviewed the six- and seven-star experiences that they came up with, they realized that they were completely doable. A guest arrives at their Airbnb where they are greeted by their host who presents them with a surfboard for their stay and confirms that they have a reservation at the most sought-after restaurant in town. Is it as grand as going to space? No. Is it much better than what the guest likely expected? You bet.

The second question involves getting the most value out of what is known as the peak-end rule. The peak-end rule is how people remember certain events or experiences. According to the Nielsen Norman Group, the peak-end rule "focuses our memories around the most intense moments of an experience and the way an experience ends."[23] If we can have a firm grasp over the most intense moments of the guest's experience, we can guide them toward the feeling of awe. By intense, we can frame that as being the emotionally impactful moments of the experience. What do you want the guest to remember most about their time with you?

To demonstrate this, we can look to Museum Hack, a tour company based in New York City, with operations throughout the United States and beyond. Museum Hack turns the world of museums upside down, acknowledging that sometimes museums can be dry and cold (both figuratively and literally). Founder Nick Gray says that he started the company to show that the museum experience can be enhanced through an entertaining, energetic, and knowledgeable guide.[24] Museum Hack hires actors and highly charismatic individuals to lead guests on unofficial museum tours. Guests can buy museum tickets through Museum Hack, and select a variety of different tour types. The tour itself is a surprise & delight experience because not every guest who visits the museum will have it; however, for Museum Hack, every one of its guests has the opportunity to be surprised and delighted through a "wow" moment. Gray reinforces this fact by challenging tour guides to ask themselves, "What's your mic-drop moment?" What can you say or do that is so powerful and impactful, that you could figuratively extend your arm completely horizontally, open up your palm and drop an imaginary microphone, letting the loud "thud" signal the jaw-dropping awe that you just delivered?

As you can see, the moments that surprise and delight your guests do not need to be a financial burden, and in some cases, they do not need to cost anything to the organization. One major advantage that hospitality, tourism, and attractions businesses have is that because so much of the product we sell is intangible, it provides the opportunity to create moments for guests that are either low cost or free, and simultaneously high value. In a world where generating revenue is usually seen as such a high priority, giving away something for free is generally frowned upon. Therefore, when determining what types of moments you should offer to your guests that will surprise and delight, I recommend breaking it down by asking the following questions:

- What do I normally charge for that, if given away for free, will have a very low cost to the business, if any?
- What is something that guests cannot normally experience during their visit that would make their day if they could?
- What do I have that goes unused during times of slower business?

- What is a common friction point in the guest experience that I can't eliminate for everybody but have the ability to do so once in a while?
- What would a VIP guest get to experience that I can occasionally pull the curtain back for a regular guest?

At a theme park, a child who is celebrating a birthday and wants to meet his or her favorite character could be accommodated with a private meet and greet, where the parents can take as many pictures as they'd like without being rushed through the process. At a zoo or aquarium, a family who expressed heightened interest in a particular animal could be taken behind the scenes and given an opportunity to feed that animal. At a bowling center, a group who is near the end of their first hour on their lane could be surprised with an additional hour added. At a hotel, a guest who indicates that it is their first visit could be granted access to the club or concierge lounge, giving them a taste of what is normally reserved for loyal guests who demonstrate repeat visitation. In any type of setting where queues form, a guest or group of guests can be selected at random and provided with expedited entry. Even smaller gestures, such as offering to take a photo of your guests and their family (whether it's to avoid the group's designated photographer not being in the pictures or to widen the frame beyond the selfie arm), is a moment that goes beyond what the guest expected to receive in that particular instance.

All of these examples have almost zero cost, if any, to the business that willingly provides them. Also, take note of how I phrased them. These moments of surprise and delight were not fueled by any specific purpose, service failure, or guest complaint. They are proactive gestures, not a reflex reaction to something unfavorable that occurred to the guest. They were done simply for the purpose of exceeding your guests' expectations so that they have an experience that was more than what they expected and more than what they paid for. These all certainly can be used for the purpose of recovering from service failures, which we will discuss in further detail in chapter 10, although they can also stand on their own as moments for your guests that drive them to loyalty.

Make a Lasting Impression on Your Guests that Extends Far Beyond Their Visit

A "WhoaZone" is like a combination of *Ninja Warrior* meets *Wipeout*. Consisting of large inflatable obstacle courses over water, guests can jump, climb, and splash for some solid family fun. To best serve multiple demographics and age groups, older kids (and those young at heart) can play on the main course while those under a certain age and height can play at the KidsZone. That means the transition from the KidsZone to the main WhoaZone can be like a rite of passage for a child who is old enough, tall enough, and most importantly, brave enough.

In one instance, there was a child who was ten or eleven years old, and he officially met the first two requirements to graduate from the KidsZone (old enough and tall enough). However, he was a bit timid to take on the larger course alone, and his parents hadn't planned on getting in the water. He wanted to do it but felt that he needed a helping hand for support. While he sat on the beach with his family debating whether he could work up the courage or whether they should just leave, a lifeguard coming back from his lunch break noticed the family in distress. Not wanting to see the guests upset, he approached the family and offered his assistance. The parents explained the circumstance, but they also told the lifeguard that he didn't need to worry about it and that they would just head home.

The lifeguard didn't worry about it. He immediately thought of a solution, and he quickly got his manager to make sure there was enough coverage in the area so he could leave his position open for a bit, then went back to the family. "Why don't I join you so you don't have to go alone, and I can make sure that you have a great time? If you're scared, I can stay with you the whole time and make sure you're comfortable. How does that sound?"

With a deep breath, the child accepted, and the parents were thrilled. For the hour that followed, something that was so simple (and fun) for that lifeguard ended up having a bigger impact than he expected when he initially offered this. The guest had a great experience, and the family was so incredibly appreciative. Because he got over such a big hurdle, the boy then craved what he was once so afraid of. The family came back multiple times that summer, which of course led to more revenue, and this family definitely proved that they were loyal.

But it was even bigger than that. Jen Rice, who oversees all of the WhoaZone locations as general manager, talked about what this "wow" moment led to. "His mom told me that after our lifeguard went with him on the WhoaZone that first time, he was then able to learn how to ride his bike. He learned how to ride his bike that summer, and she attributed it to us helping him to overcome that fear. It gave me that warm fuzzy feeling that our lifeguard was able to go play for an hour with one of our guests. It really impacted this child and their entire family."[25]

You never know what type of impact you can make on the lives of your guests and their families, and how it can have such a positive impression on other aspects of their lives. It can be building courage like this example showed, inspiring someone to learn more about a particular topic and influencing someone's career path, or bringing a family closer together who may be experiencing a hardship. In this case, the lifeguard saw an opportunity that went beyond what the guest expected, that went beyond what his job duty required, that did not upset any other guest, and that cost absolutely nothing to deliver. He hit all four points, and it worked flawlessly.

Because the second step is that it goes beyond the staff member's job duties, what if he didn't do this? His job description would suggest that he would come back from break, clock back in, and resume his post. It's not like this was a recovery from a service failure. Nothing from an operational standpoint had actually gone wrong; this frustration was manufactured by the guest 100 percent. They could have gone home instead, and it wouldn't have been WhoaZone's fault or the fault of any employee who had interacted with them. Projecting out this alternate reality further, the child wouldn't have learned to ride his bike that summer, he would be behind in general when developing courage, and the family certainly wouldn't have come back. They might also tell other people that they didn't have a good experience, and even though they wouldn't have any negative comments about Whoa-Zone in general, it still would count as negative word of mouth because it would give the message that it's a scary experience, rather than the fun and thrilling time that WhoaZone intended to communicate and set as an expectation.

If you are in a position where you have to consider whether the "wow" moment will be worth it or not, ask, "What will happen if we don't decide to do this?" The guest isn't expecting it anyway, so you can't be faulted if you don't go that extra mile. But then, follow that up by asking, "What will happen if we *do* decide to do this?" Now you can start projecting out all of the possible positive outcomes that can come from implementing "wow" moments that go far beyond the guest's expectations. As we move toward the third section of the book, which will lead to driving guest loyalty, it's much easier to lead a guest to loyalty if they've had a "wow" experience than a guest who had a satisfactory one. While loyalty is fostered in the postvisit, it is what you do throughout the duration of the visit that will formulate how they reflect on their experience once it's complete. And the best way to stack the deck in your favor is by creating "wow" moments that they can't help but dwell on, talk about, and shout from the rooftops—or at least post online.

The instant a guest makes contact with your organization, whether it is the first foot they step in the door or any previsit communication they may have with your staff, this is the first moment of truth. These moments of truth continue throughout the full duration of the visit, with every staff member who interacts with them while on-site, and continue beyond the visit if they contact you about their previous experience, or whether they are gearing up for their next one. Every moment of truth is an opportunity to exceed your guests' expectations. Every moment of truth is a chance to go above and beyond what the guest expected, knowing that the expectation was considerably high, otherwise, they would have gone elsewhere, done something different, or opted to do nothing at all. And if we know that every moment of truth is a chance to exceed expectations, it also means that with every moment of truth there is a chance of a service failure as well. That choice, and that control, lie substantially with the individuals who are delivering the experience to your guests. With all of the moments of truth that a guest encounters throughout their visit, their overall level of satisfaction will be determined by how well each moment of truth went beyond their expectation, and the positive differential between expectation and reality in those moments must be greater than the negative differential of any service failures that may have occurred, otherwise, the likelihood of loyalty substantially drops . . .

. . . unless you do something about it. Part 3 will take us beyond the initial guest experience, and revisit what we need from a guest in order to ensure lifelong loyalty, what actions you must take in order to look back and recognize how well you did in providing an exceptional experience, and what you must do to influence the loyalty actions that were outlined in chapter 2.

Chapter 8 Strategy Statement:

Whenever we can, we create "wow" moments that surprise and delight our guests and go far beyond even their highest expectations.

PART 3:

PUT FUEL ON THE FIRE

At this stage in the guest journey, we have determined the expectations and reviewed what needs to be done to meet them, and then we focused on creative ways to exceed expectations that can be built into your operating model. Now, considering our goal of loyalty, we want to push ourselves further by putting systems in place that occur toward the end of a guest's duration of their visit and into the postvisit that guide them toward our actions of loyalty—they return, they influence others to visit, and they stick up for you.

Too often, businesses will focus on providing a great experience and assume that loyalty will happen naturally. In a perfect world, we would set an expectation for our guests and then exceed it, and it will automatically turn every guest into an advocate. However, we know that every guest is unique, which means that their expectations differ, and so do the perceptions of their individual experiences. Because of this, we must continue to tailor the journey by identifying who the guest is, how the experience compared with their expectation, and then acting from there.

There are multiple permutations that we can consider: the guest expected **x**, experienced **y**, and we respond with **z**. And yes, there should *always* be a z.

Not to be too heavy on the math, but if x is greater than y, the guest senses a service failure, and z will equate to service recovery. This recovery will focus on increasing y so that it is now greater than x, where we can now influence our loyalty drivers of repeat visitation and positive word of mouth. If y is greater than x, then z equates to influencing our loyalty drivers, skipping over service recovery. To put this more simply, intercept your dissatisfied guests and convert them into satisfied, and take your satisfied guests (even if they were initially dissatisfied) and push them toward loyalty.

But what if x = y? In this case, we're left with a neutrally satisfied guest whose experience met the expectation exactly, which doesn't help us at all. Will they come back? We don't know. Will they tell others? We don't know. We didn't fall below their expectation, but we didn't go beyond either. Yet we still need to solve for z. To do this, we need to know who falls into which camp. Unless guests tell you directly, how do you know who is satisfied and who is dissatisfied? This is where many businesses don't take the effort to drive the guest experience further. If a guest comes and goes without any indicator of their level of satisfaction—including leaving feedback or posting a review—we turn them loose into the world when we could have kept them in our realm.

This section will cover the following:

- **Chapter 9: Optimize Your Feedback Loop:** strategize feedback with guest communication, and use the data to initiate change

- **Chapter 10: Recover from Service Failures:** recognize that missing the mark is not the end of the world when managed properly
- **Chapter 11: Set Wheels in Motion:** influence repeat visitation and positive word of mouth through effective post-visit guest engagement
- **Chapter 12: Celebrate Every Guest:** do this with every guest, every time, and the Hospitality Mentality will breed more loyal guests organically

Chapter 9:
Optimize Your Feedback Loop

———— 🍍 ————

I n the spring of 2010, The Wizarding World of Harry Potter
opened at Universal Orlando Resort and was an immediate
booming success. Due to the intense passion toward the brand
that encompassed the globe, hordes of guests arrived on the day of
the grand opening of this new "theme park within a theme park,"
and the popularity only grew further throughout the summer and
into the holiday season. There was a definitive shift in the land-
scape of the resort and the guest experience, and my role at the
time was deep in the trenches of guest feedback.

At the time, I was a senior coordinator for the resort's Guest
Communications team, a small but mighty division of the Guest
Services department. Any company's Guest Communications
team acts as the outlet to which guests should have the ability to
vent, and then the venting needs to be translated into actionable,
unbiased data that is organized and distributed to each department and categorized based on the nature of the feedback. One
unit of guest feedback stands on its own. Unless there is a glaring
risk management liability, one unit of feedback should be dealt
with swiftly and then filed accordingly, relative to all other feed-

back received within a consistently measured timeframe. It is then through tracking *aggregated quantifiable demand* that you can quickly highlight priorities to determine what changes need to be addressed urgently.

Part of my job was to take the massive amounts of feedback that we got each week, turn the narratives into data, and then highlight the biggest issues that would rise to the surface. This was all summarized in a weekly report that was sent to senior leadership across the entire resort. It was an arduous process that would involve assigning metrics to every single thing a guest would comment on (whether positive or negative), and then making sense of the thousands of data points so that proper action could be taken.

What does this have to do with Harry Potter? Because of the seismic shift that The Wizarding World of Harry Potter brought to the resort, the nature of guest feedback changed entirely as well. In particular, one of the most popular retail products were magic wands that aligned exactly with how they were described in the books and presented in the movies. Even the manner in which wands are sold is a heightened experience compared to a regular gift shop, with immersive entertainment that enhanced the "shopping" experience . . . if you can even call it shopping.

The wands were understandably popular from day one, with both adults and children, which also meant that the purpose of the product would be defined differently by each user. For the mega Harry Potter fan, the wand would most likely end up on display in their home, perhaps in a stand on the mantel or even placed in a glass case; this was as much a collectible as it was a souvenir. For the younger crowd though? Give two kids a $30 stick each and time how long it takes for the wands to turn into lightsabers.

One of the largest complaints received after this new land opened was that wands broke too easily. Despite there being a small label on the box indicating that this product is "not a toy," our office quickly became inundated with broken wands that needed to be replaced and shipped back to guests. Our team would manage this, at no cost to the guest, and we would even reimburse their shipping costs for sending it back to us. The process for service recovery was effective for guests on an individual basis, but not sustainable. If nothing was done, guests would continue to be dissatisfied, merchandise would regularly continue to be replaced, and the energy of the Guest Communications team would be focused more on replacing wands than it would be on serving guests.

We needed to optimize our feedback loop. But what does that even mean?

Your Guests Aren't Complaining Enough

Part of seeking feedback is striving to increase the volume of guest complaints. When complaints are received internally, rather than online, they provide the intelligence that the business needs in order to make improvements. You need to show your guests that you want to know where the friction is by asking them directly.

Alamo Rent a Car does this well. Whenever I rent a car with Alamo, upon returning the car, I have noticed that the agent goes through the functional points of inspecting the car, checking the mileage, and ensuring that everything has been removed, and then prompts me with "What can we do to make your rental experience better in the future?" This is the perfect opportunity to request feedback while the guest is still in front of you, leaving you with the ability to document their concerns and rectify any issues at that moment. In fact, I feel bad when I *don't* have a complaint! If you can make your guests feel bad for *not* complaining, then you know you are optimizing guest feedback better than your industry standard. When we operate under the mindset that we cannot reach the peak of the guest experience, we can always work toward making improvements for the next guest.

How Do You Get Guest Feedback?

In chapter 2, we reviewed the categories of satisfaction: your guests should be categorized as either **promoters** or **detractors**. Your **promoters** are the ones you can count on. If you successfully exceeded their expectations through one or more of the strategies in part 2, you are stacking the deck in your favor to produce more promoters. They are working on your behalf to *promote* your business through positive word of mouth, favorable online reviews, and regularly weaving your business into conversations and shining a positive light.

Since this is a binary segmentation, **detractors** are your guests whom you failed. Their expectations were not met, and as a result, they are vocally speaking out *against* your business. Through negative word of mouth and angry online reviews, detractors are not only guests that you have lost—they are seeing to it that others avoid your business as well. For the same reason that promoters produce more promoters, detractors will produce more detractors, and what makes matters worse is that detractors reproduce at a higher rate than promoters. Negative experiences are shared far more than positive experiences, meaning that your detractors will hurt your business more than promoters will help it.

By continually gaining awareness of promoters and detractors, you can take swift action to minimize the reputational damage that your detractors can cause. For instance, one of your top priorities in the realm of feedback collection should be boosting your rating and ranking on online review sites; however, you must segment your guests into promoter and detractor categories *before* focusing on your online review presence, and *only* push your promoters to review sites while taking immediate action to convert your detractors. Segmenting your guests allows you to control the direction you would like their feedback to be directed. There are too many businesses across nearly every industry that use social media and online reviews as their primary form of feedback collection. While this may provide information that they need to hear, it also is a gamble that cannot guarantee how their business will be perceived by online audiences. This is risky because the online audience is made up of impressionable people who are using past experiences of other guests to help determine whether they will visit you or not. Feedback from previous guests is a huge part of defining the expectation for guests who have yet to visit.

The way that your guests provide their feedback after their visit is going to determine the future success of your business. According to a survey in 2016, 90 percent of purchase decisions are heavily impacted by online reviews.[26] Therefore, segmenting your guests into categories of *satisfied* and *dissatisfied* can optimize your chances of gaining more positive reviews and minimize people airing your dirty laundry. Before pushing people online, you want to seek feedback through internal channels, rather than reading their thoughts for the first time in the public domain.

There are many ways to collect feedback from your guests, either during their visit or shortly after, that can give you crucial information. Postvisit emails or text messages, survey kiosks, and even traditional comment cards are all ways to collect both qualitative and quantitative data. These can provide great information for how you continually improve the experience for future guests, using guest feedback as the primary market research tool. Guest feedback should carry a high weight in your overall business strategy. What to add, what to remove, what to change, what new products to offer, and what marketing promotions to run can all be determined by studying guest perceptions and taking note of where the gaps are. However, there is one that they cannot always do: give you the opportunity to take action with that guest in real time.

It is crucial to open up the communication channels for your guests to provide feedback to you to avoid any bottlenecks in feedback that should be given but is too difficult for the guest to provide. Collecting feedback begins with actively generating feedback while on-site, then requesting feedback internally after a visit, and lastly by leveraging online reviews. It is crucial that these steps are completed in order so you can rectify issues in real time, segment your guests into promoters and detractors, and then push your promoters online while retaining control over the conversation with your detractors. Let's review each of the three steps in greater detail.

3 STEPS FOR SOLICITING GUEST FEEDBACK

COLLECT FEEDBACK WHILE ON-SITE   REQUEST FEEDBACK INTERNALLY   LEVERAGE ONLINE REVIEWS

Step 1: Collect Feedback While On-site

It is much better to take care of an issue while the guest is still on-site when there is still an opportunity to salvage a negative experience, rather than scrambling to regain confidence postvisit. To be proactive when collecting feedback, the most basic strategies are usually the most effective. This is where the *hospitality* component of the Hospitality Mentality comes into play. Ask your guests how they're doing. Ask them whether they enjoyed their visit or experience, or whether they are enjoying themselves at that time. Ask them whether there was something that could have made their visit or experience better. What their most memorable aspect was. Whether they have visited before and how this visit compared to any previous experiences. Whether they have visited your competitors and how their experience visiting you differs or what similarities there are. Whether they are likely to visit again. In the aforementioned Alamo example, the agent will specifically ask for ways that they can improve, giving the guest the stage to make a complaint right then and there, without being labeled as a complainer.

Take a page or two from chapter 5, and personalize the experience to the highest degree possible. All frontline and guest-facing staff members should have "actively seeking feedback on a personal level" as part of their job description, alongside all of the actions toward providing an experience that exceeds expectations. Regularly asking guests about their experience at frequent points *during* their visit, and certainly near the *end* of their experience, gives you the opportunity to either correct the course or set the wheels in motion toward loyalty, both of which will be discussed in the next chapters.

Step 2: Request Feedback Internally (Postvisit)

As the experience ends, all of the moments of truth are added up to determine whether the experience exceeded or fell below expectation. The most important thing to remember in this case is that even though the experience is over, *they are still your guest*. This may not always sound intuitive as they are no longer on your premises and no longer spending money, but they are still within the framework of the guest experience cycle. Because most guests are not going to provide feedback unless they are prompted to do so (and even then, most guests still won't), this is where the assumption lies of neutral satisfaction.

In order to request feedback after a visit, you must have a means of doing so. It is much easier to do so nowadays, with reservations being made in advance or purchases being made online, where guest contact data is required to make a purchase, but not every business has their guests' information. A restaurant, for example, does not automatically gain a guest's email address unless there is a specific reason to do so. It is the job of the operator then to provide that reason, such as through a reservation made online or through the guest joining a rewards program by adding their email address or phone number to their signed check at the end of their meal. As we know, a rewards program is *not* a loyalty program, but it is the steppingstone to loyalty. A rewards program should be used to deepen relationships with your guests so you can continue to serve them beyond their initial visit, but you cannot look at the size of your email list and call that the size of your loyal following. Gaining your guests' contact information by providing rewards for future visits is part of the process, but it will never be the process in its entirety.

One of the first pieces of communication that the guest should receive is a prompt for feedback. This can be done through surveys to collect quantitative data, as well as through open-ended questions that provide qualitative data. Oftentimes, businesses will assume that the quantitative data is more important due to the ease of aggregation, but there must be a mix of numbers and narratives to provide a full, accurate picture. Even though narrative responses present greater difficulty with identifying trends, they give the guest the chance to tell you what they thought was important, and which key performance indicators (KPIs) you should be measuring. If you ask your guests a list of preset questions in a lengthy survey, you run the risk of survey fatigue, which results in guests opting out of the survey early, or you lack the context to the numbers, which means the data will show vague understandings of which areas of your business rank lower than others.

Your internal feedback should be responded to swiftly, whether it is in the form of an email, survey, letter, private message on social media, or other means that the guest has taken to get information directly to you, regardless of sentiment. If the guest calls, their call should be answered quickly, demonstrating an effective Guest Communications team that knows that the guest is still the guest, even if they are not on-site at that time. Electronic messaging, including email, text, or app-based communication should regularly be monitored. According to a survey conducted by Arise in 2019, 37 percent of customers expect a response to an email *within one hour* of sending it.[27] Are you prepared for that quick response time? The longer that correspondence sits unanswered, the more frustrated your guests get. The quicker you respond, the better chance you have to turn this into a "wow" moment.

Step 3: Leverage Online Reviews

Similar to internal feedback, online reviews should be responded to quickly. Your online reviews should be treated similarly to your internal feedback, as they are generally blocks of narrative response where the guest shares what was important to their individual experience. This differs from surveys where guests are prompted to rank certain factors because in this case the guest brings you the KPIs that are the most important to them. By extracting these KPIs and turning them into quantitative metrics, you can effectively turn your qualitative information into quantitative, and with online reviews, you can apply the same principles to your competitors to conduct a competitive analysis with an apples-to-apples comparison. If no other similar businesses in your region saw nearly as many complaints related to say, price perception, as yours did over the previous month, you can see that you're the problem.

Keep in mind that online reviews are both a blessing and a curse; your promoters should be using these platforms to reinforce the decision to visit you for those who may be on the fence or doing their research. This is where your promoters become an extension of your marketing team, as they help begin the guest experience cycle anew for your next guest that you get to wow. Your detractors, on the other hand, may naturally gravitate to these platforms for vengeance if they feel that they have been wronged in any way during the course of their visit. This is particularly true for guests who have a tendency to provide feedback only in polarizing circumstances and prefer posting online versus telling you in person. While this hopefully is a small subset of the majority of the guests you serve, their voice will be louder than the promoters. It is your job to make sure that the promoters have their platform to sing your praises while you privately rectify issues for your detractors away from the spotlight.

The purpose of both steps 1 and 2 is to *reduce*, not eliminate, negative online reviews from being posted. You cannot stop a dissatisfied guest from leaving a scathing review, but the more barriers you put in their way gives you a greater chance to intervene with a guest who had a bad experience. Internal feedback collection is your layer of protection between a bad experience and a bad review.

What Do We Do with All This Data?

One reason for guest feedback data collection is to deepen your relationships with your guests and to foster guest loyalty, regardless of whether the guest is satisfied or dissatisfied. From an internal standpoint, this data must be used to initiate change to improve your organization. These changes should benefit future guests, as well as operational improvements that support your frontline staff, and ultimately help to enhance the guest experience, business operations, and growth of profitability.

Once you identify what the glaring issues are through aggregating the data, correcting them can become a challenge on their own. Guests will often present a problem, but they might not be the best ones to recommend the solution. The solutions are usually not the most obvious ones either. That is why it is important to pull back from only looking at what the problem actually is and start looking at it through the lens of the guest experience. You and your team need to be asking, *what is the guest actually complaining about?*

Let's revisit the example from the beginning of this chapter regarding the wands from The Wizarding World of Harry Potter. The issue was addressed directly in the weekly comment report, but it was important that it not be buried in a mountain of data. There needed to be the narrative in the report that indicated that young guests are not reading the "not a toy" label and nor are their parents, therefore these novel wands are coming back in droves.

The leaders of the retail department were able to take quick action, including increasing the visibility of the "not a toy" label and communicating this with their management, supervisors, and frontline staff members. By bringing this to the staff's attention, they were able to effectively *anticipate guests' needs* and answer the question that would rarely be asked: *do these wands break easily?*

Even though it would rarely be asked, the staff now had the proficiency to be proactive and specifically point out the "not a toy" label and say something like, "Just letting you know, this is fragile. Be careful when casting spells."

If we looked at the issue at face value, we would come to the conclusion that "wand = flimsy," and that these complaints would stop if we were able to make "wand = sturdy"; therefore, selling a more durable product. There would have been calls back and forth with the manufacturer, new product specifications, increased cost of the product (resulting in either lower profit margins or an increase in retail price—negatively impacting the guest experience), placing new orders that were not planned, and attempting to liquidate the old product. In the time that this would take to accomplish, in the midst of the busiest summer the resort had ever seen to date, the Guest Communications team would still be fielding these complaints on a daily basis, shipping new wands for free, and getting nowhere with solving this massive service failure.

Instead, the retail management took an operational approach that involved no immediate changes to the product. Repositioning the label was a much easier task than reengineering the product, and incorporating the verbiage into the language of the frontline staff allowed parents of small children to take a moment and say to themselves, "Oh yeah. This thing can break easily, so I'd better make sure my kid isn't swinging it around at everything. It wasn't cheap, and I want to make sure it lasts."

Once this change was made, the Guest Communications team replaced far fewer wands, leaving the team with more time to focus on that next guest and their feedback, and saving the company a substantial amount of money that was being spent on replacing the wands. By measuring the reduction in broken wands that were returned, we were able to follow the data and report back as to what was working and what could decrease the complaints even further.

We optimized the feedback loop. We used what guests were saying and made small changes that had significant positive impacts.

Optimizing your feedback loop is not intended to eliminate guests' concerns entirely, but by using the data from your most important resource—your guests—you can identify what necessary changes and updates should be your topmost priority. When you tackle your priorities and implement changes, any rift in new procedures will be met with some degree of resistance, which is why it is critical to continue measuring guest feedback on a regular basis with regular reporting, such as daily, weekly, monthly, quarterly, and annually to compartmentalize blocks of time to note upward and downward trends. By keeping your finger on the pulse of these scores, you can continually refine your operations to strive toward continuous improvement. This is an exciting challenge because it is never finished; that's why guest feedback is a loop. It is continually coming in as you continue to make your guest experience even better for your future guests.

Now, let's take a look at the best ways to bounce back when the experience that the guest had did not meet their expectation prior to their visit.

Chapter 9 Strategy Statement:

We seek and embrace guest feedback as the driving force for continually improving the experience.

Chapter 10:
Recover from Service Failures

———— 🍍 ————

"What are we doing to make sure that we have no guest complaints?"

That's what my manager asked me after getting my third complaint in a month. It was the park's first full month of operation, and we were still working the kinks out. I had been planning for the park's opening for seven months before the ribbon-cutting, giving me ample time to put together a guest experience strategy that ensured that we could deliver on our promises and then execute the strategies for exceeding expectations as discussed in each chapter from part 2. Our orientation and training included how we were going to meet expectations, personalize the experience, maintain enthusiasm, anticipate needs, and deliver "wow" moments at every possible opportunity. I had a team of about fifty employees who were all hired for their personality and their ability to deliver on this standard.

If that was the case, why did my department get three guest complaints within the first month of the park's opening? We were being as proactive as possible to minimize the likelihood of service failures, and we regularly received high praise through internal feedback and on social media. However, it's the guest who determines their level of satisfaction. Perception is reality, and sometimes the guest's perception will differ from yours. You will often receive complaints that you don't agree with, or where the guest may have been misinformed or even have been outright wrong, but that doesn't make the complaints any less significant.

For each of the complaints I received that flagged my manager's attention, there were actually two benefits. The first relates to what we did with the feedback and how we used it to make ongoing improvements to the guest experience. The second was how we were able to repair, and even strengthen, the relationship we had with the guests who complained. By effectively resolving their issues, their satisfaction was even higher at the end of it because of the emotional peaks and valleys that they traveled. They sent an email out of frustration, and then they were contacted by me—someone who could fix it, but even more than that, someone who was on their side and wasn't there to argue with them. These negative circumstances led to extremely positive outcomes.

Extensive research has been conducted on service failures across a wide variety of industries, and this even has a specific name: **the recovery paradox**.[28] The recovery paradox suggests that when a consumer has an experience that dissatisfied them, and when they speak up and have their dissatisfaction resolved, their satisfaction on the other side is even higher than consumers who reported that they were fully satisfied with their purchase. While this does not suggest that you should intentionally build service failures into your guest experience, it gives assurance that when a guest complains, not only is it not the end of the world but it's also an opportunity to create a "wow" moment.

So how did I respond to this manager? I said, "Actually, we're not getting enough complaints." Every time a guest complains, the guest experience gets stronger in the long run, and we've been given the opportunity to make someone's day. If more guests complained, or at least offered constructive feedback about their visit, then there is no stopping how much we can grow from it. Further research has indicated that only one out of twenty-six people who have a complaint will speak up.[29] The other twenty-five will accept that they are dissatisfied and most likely won't come back due to their experience. For every complaint you resolve, think about the other twenty-five guests who had the same issue and said nothing.

Service recovery, when delivered successfully, will be even more memorable than the complaint itself. When you provide recovery after a service failure, it shows the guest that you are prepared to fix a problem when it presents itself. It shows that there is a sincere human element that cares and is empathetic to the guest experience. Take a look at your online reviews. If you find a positive review that indicates a problem that was solved, in many cases, it will have a more enthusiastic tone than other high-rated reviews. In fact, these reviews may be specifically referring to the recovery, rather than the issue itself. In many cases, they may refer to the manager or the staff member who assisted them in correcting their issue. Use these situations to your advantage. Service recovery is a form of surprising and delighting your guests. Even though it is reactive to negative situations, it becomes a "wow" moment that can have incredible impacts when done correctly.

The LAST Model

Your team members must be equipped with the proper skills for addressing complaints and solving them. The best way to eliminate the phrase "Let me get my manager" is to provide your frontline staff with the training to address complaints and the tools that they can use to recover from service failures. When an employee has to escalate a situation to leadership, everyone feels frustrated. The guest feels it because now the process has been prolonged and they'll probably need to repeat themselves, the employee is frustrated because now their routine has been disrupted by a disgruntled guest whom they can't help, and the manager is frustrated because now they probably have other things competing for their attention and resources. The training and the recovery toolbox can eliminate this frustration.

Building an operation that includes recovering from service failures is vital to the health of your business. If you are serving hundreds, thousands, or tens of thousands of people per day, and you believe that you can perfectly deliver your intended guest experience to each and every one, every single time, then you are living in a false reality. While that should certainly be the ultimate goal, you always need a fallback plan. Effective service recovery is that plan. And fortunately, just like the elements of exceeding guests' expectations, there is a structured accordion-style approach to service recovery, referred to as the LAST model, that can be applied from the smallest of inconveniences to some of the most complex service failures, and everything in between. The LAST model is as much of a science as it is an art. The LAST approach, similar to several other methods of diffusing a negative situation, has evolved over the years, with many experts adding their input and interpretation. I have always found this model to be the easiest to remember and implement, and also the most effective when done in the specific order that it is presented. Here is the breakdown of each step of the LAST model, which can be defined as **Listen**, **Apologize**, **Solve**, and **Thank**.

LAST MODEL

LISTEN

APOLOGIZE

SOLVE

THANK

Step 1: Listen

While it seems so fundamental, the first step in a complaint resolution process is to listen to your guests' concerns. When someone has something to say, sometimes they just want to be heard. For some people, this is the only step they care about. They may even suggest that they are not looking for any type of compensation, but rather they feel fulfilled just knowing that they have communicated their feedback to someone who will listen. Giving them that opportunity might be 90 percent of the resolution process.

Listening also incorporates body language. Focus on the guest without any distractions to show that you are truly invested in the conversation. If the guest is complaining in person and you are in a noisy environment, relocate to a quiet area if you have the ability to do so. Maintain eye contact, don't interrupt, and keep a concerned look on your face, nodding your head occasionally to show that you are on the same page. If you are speaking with the guest over the phone, you do not have the benefits of eye contact and body language, but your vocal cues can indicate the same effect. Offering an occasional "I understand" or even "mm-hmm" shows the guest that you are there, taking it in, and in agreement.

Show the guest that you understand. Repeat the concern back to the guest in your words, concisely communicating back the points that the guest is making, eliminating any fluff. Provide them with your interpretation of their concern, and give the guest the opportunity to affirm your response, or correct you if needed, at which point you must repeat this process. By engaging in dialogue to confirm that you are aware of their specific concerns, you turn the process from passive listening into active listening.

Additionally, one of the most important aspects of listening includes validation. If you are reading this and have ever served guests in some capacity, you probably hate the saying "The customer is always right." I agree, because many times, they simply aren't. Oftentimes guests will complain about something that is not truly complaint-worthy, or perhaps they were misinformed. During the listening phase, it is not the time to point that out. Instead of plastering that unfavorable maxim on the breakroom bulletin board, use this alternative: *let the guest be right, even if they're wrong*. Suggesting that the guest is incorrect does not pave the way for a successful resolution process. Let's say, for instance, that the guest indicated that your facility was unclean, when in fact your cleanliness standards indicate otherwise, along with a review of surveillance tapes that showed no trash on the ground during the time of their visit. If their perception differed from what you believe to be the reality, they will still carry that with them, and that is what will translate into negative word of mouth and online reviews. At that point, does it even matter if they were right or wrong?

While listening, thank the guest for complaining. Before moving on to the next step, I want to touch on appreciating the guest's concern, as the bridge between listening and apologizing. Once you have listened, understood, and validated the guest's complaint, you want to show your appreciation to them for providing the feedback. A single complaint may be the voice of many others, and it is imperative to show that you appreciate that they took the time to complain. When you say, "First and foremost, I want to thank you so much for bringing this to our attention," you immediately tear down a wall that existed between you and the guest. If the complaint is severe, the guest is most likely heated, and they are prepared to argue. Thanking the guest at this step in the process keeps you in the driver's seat.

When you thank the guest for complaining, you show them that you are the one who is going to fix the problem and that you aren't going to fight about it. You are demonstrating ownership of the situation, and by thanking the guest before you have even done anything, it makes the rest of the process much smoother. I have encountered and observed numerous situations where a guest was so upset that it seemed that their issue was completely unsolvable. The guest was allowed however much time they needed to vent their concerns, while I listened intently, took notes, and only spoke a few words of validation to let them know that I was actively listening. Then, upon finishing, I thanked them for their concerns and for bringing them to my attention. There would then be a notable sigh of relief, and you could feel the tension starting to diminish. This was prior to any apology being given and the resolution had not even been discussed. By showing that the guest's concern was not only heard, but understood, validated, and appreciated, the flames were mostly put out, allowing the remainder of the steps to fall in line quite nicely. **Do not skip this step. Always express appreciation when a guest complains.**

Step 2: Apologize

Just like listening, apologizing for a service failure might seem like a simple, rote function as you race to the solution step, when in actuality, it must be carefully delivered in order for it to be effective, and just like listening and appreciating, must all be completed in the correct order. In this step, the key to remember is that this is an expression of empathy, not an admission of fault, nor is it placing blame in any direction. In order to determine the correct and incorrect ways to apologize, we must first identify the two main types of complaints: subjective perceptions or potential liabilities.

Subjective perception. These types of complaints are when the guest tells you how they perceived their experience. Factors like service, cleanliness, enjoyment, wait time, crowds, and food temperature are generally going to differ based on what the guest expects, which as we know, will vary from one guest to another. Guests perceive things in different ways. When you look at your online reviews, you may see one review that praises your facility for excellent service and being immaculate, while the next review may say the exact opposite, and those guests may have visited on the same day at the same time. Based on the expectation that the guest is carrying with them when they arrive, the perception of their experience will be subjectively different from other guests around them. A one-hour wait may seem like an eternity, or it may seem reasonable, depending on how that guest perceived it before getting in line.

In these instances, your apology must reflect that the guest is providing you with their opinion, and it must be treated as such. If you apologize that your facility is dirty, you are taking the blame for it and admitting fault. If you apologize that a team member was rude, you are admitting that they in fact were providing poor service. Instead, align your apology with how the guest communicated the complaint with what your standard is. Phrase it in a way that validates the guest's concern, but does not guarantee that it occurred. For example, an apology for a subjective perception should sound along the lines of the following: "We expect full commitment from our team members, and ***what you described*** does not meet our standards." This sentence was carefully constructed and phrased intentionally. The words "what you described" keep the conversation about what the guest has communicated to you, rather than on what potentially occurred. You are giving them the benefit of the doubt that they are correct, although you never actually admit that it happened. Instead, you are saying that if it did happen, it shouldn't have, because it does not meet your standard.

Potential liability. These are complaints that cannot be disputed, nor will their perception vary from one guest to the next. They are facts, not opinions. Something was not operating, either due to technical or operational reasons, when it was expected to be functioning. A guest tripped on an unmarked curb and sprained their ankle. A cash register malfunctioned, cutting efficiency in half. The security tag wasn't removed from clothing at the point of purchase. The guest was unable to enjoy the experience due to the weather. A guest's car was broken into in the parking lot. In these situations, these are potential liabilities, either due to potential legal consequences or at the very minimum they can still impact a guest's desire to visit again and can result in word of mouth that can damage your reputation.

Similar to a subjective perception complaint, a complaint revolving around a potential liability also should avoid recognition that it occurred. If you say, "I am so sorry that you tripped and fell on our unmarked curb and sprained your ankle," you not only accept blame but you are inviting a possible lawsuit. Instead, *apologize for the effect, rather than the cause,* in these types of situations. What happened as a result of this incident that relates to the guest experience? For all of the examples provided above, there is one overarching statement that can apply. Take note of the words that are marked in bold and italics for emphasis: "I am sorry that you did not get to ***enjoy your visit as you expected***." It is important to recognize that this statement expresses empathy for how the negative situation impacted their experience visiting you, rather than apologizing for what specifically occurred. From an initial service recovery standpoint, this is not the time to address the cause, but rather the effect that you can solve. You are resolving an issue related to their experience, and your apology should reflect that. Similarly, other effective apologetic statements can include, "I apologize that you had to leave early," "I apologize for any inconvenience that may have occurred during your visit," or "Please be assured that we would never intentionally inconvenience our guests." Leaving early and being inconvenienced are effects, and therefore they can be apologized for, and your apology does not need to acknowledge the cause in order to be effective.

When it comes to making an effective apology, we now know the details in the phrasing and the words used when expressing empathy. There is one word, however, that usually finds its way into service recovery communication that should be eliminated entirely. That word is *unfortunately*. When you use the word "unfortunately," you appear as if you are apologizing for a policy, and you are disconnecting yourself from the issue, and in many cases, from the company as a whole. It makes you sound like you would take care of an issue if you could, but you can't, so you aren't going to. Here are a few examples:

- Unfortunately, we have a no refund policy.
- Unfortunately, we don't provide rain checks.
- Unfortunately, it's very crowded because we have a lot of groups visiting today.
- Unfortunately, they raised our prices recently.
- Unfortunately, we don't have cameras in our parking lot.

Did you cringe while you read each of those? Not one of these statements sound friendly, hospitable, or empathetic. Eliminate "unfortunately" from your vocabulary, and instead focus on what you *can* do, as you move into an effective resolution.

Step 3: Solve

Solving a guest's issue is only one of the steps in the resolution process. While it may be considered the most important, it is imperative to follow the LAST model in order so that the recovery is the most effective. Otherwise, jumping to the solution makes it appear to be a knee-jerk reaction that lacks the hospitality and attention that it deserves. This entire process is meant to be expanded or contracted if necessary, depending on the size and severity of the complaint. Listening and apologizing can take ten seconds or ten minutes, depending on the complexity, although they must still be completed before resolution takes place. When it comes to resolving service failures of various degrees, here are three guidelines: always give them something, the recovery should fit the failure, and require the guest to return.

Always give them something. This statement may sound bold. It usually raises an eyebrow when I present it at conferences or workshops. However, if you create the proper recovery options for your staff to provide, you can maintain control. This is where the nature of the product you sell comes to your advantage. So much of what you deliver is intangible, which means there is a high value to the guest, yet minimal—if any—cost to the business. Look to "wow" moments as your guide, where you can surprise and delight your guests with the intangible value that you offer. Everything that you have mapped out that can be delivered to a guest as a "wow" moment is now available as a recovery tool as well. The personal escort that can eliminate the wait time, the behind-the-scenes look, and the quick meet and greet with the child's favorite characters are all high-value deliverables that have almost no cost to the company.

When you implement the *always give them something* rule, you show your commitment to the hospitable service culture. You are not afraid to go above and beyond for the guest when duty calls. Additionally, when you offer, and the guest accepts, your service recovery, this can be considered closure on that issue. If the guest takes the complaint public, you can respond with how you addressed their concern, which is better than not having offered anything.

Always ensure that you verify the concern to the best of your ability, document their feedback properly, and track any compensation given. The *always give them something* rule means that you might be conditioning guests to complain, which should work out to your benefit if the complaints are constructive. If guests begin to complain because they know they'll get something, you'll want to ensure that you have tracked their communication over time, and if it becomes excessive, you'll have the justification to cut them off. While this is not always the most comfortable of situations, you may occasionally have to red flag a guest if it appears that they might be trying to take advantage of you.

The recovery should fit the failure. This is about making it an even trade, or at least as even as possible. If x went wrong, solve for x. If the guest tells you that a wait time was longer than expected, do what you can to make up for the lost time. If a meal was prepared incorrectly, replace it with the correct meal. If the guest complains that it is too crowded, and if you have a way of helping them circumvent the crowds and even help them plan their day accordingly, do what you can do to get them out of the crowd. A spilled popcorn warrants a new popcorn, not a night in the presidential suite of a five-star hotel. Overcompensating service failures is when "always give them something" can run off the rails.

When looking to surprise and delight your guests with effective service recovery, you must also exercise the anticipation of your guests' needs and look beyond what the guest is complaining about, factoring in any ancillary service failures that surround what went wrong. For example, let's say a guest's credit card was double charged and they realized it a few days after their visit. The proper recovery is to reverse the duplicate charge, but what if the guest used a debit card and it resulted in an overdraft? Then, when they called to inform of you the issue, what if they waited on hold for an hour? Now there are three service failures that warrant recovery: the card being charged twice, an overdraft fee, and one hour of time that needs to be replaced. You must go beyond the initial complaint and acknowledge that service failures sometimes create a domino effect.

Require the guest to return. This is where service recovery can truly work in your favor and turn negative situations into future revenue. Offer compensation that will go into effect on their *next* visit. If a guest says that they waited an extensive amount of time for a table in your restaurant, you can offer priority seating next time. If they express concern about food quality, show them that you will address their concerns with your culinary team, and offer to replace their meal when they come back in the future. If crowds are an issue and you have a form of expedited access to avoid crowds, consider providing that at no cost when the guest returns.

Even if you provide compensation upfront that is fulfilled immediately, consider sweetening the pot by telling them how their next experience will be better. This demonstrates the value of the compensation that the guest receives, thus making the recovery paradox more likely, but it also benefits the business in the end. If you offer a free meal for a guest on their next visit, they will probably still be likely to spend money with you somehow. In destination theme parks, the amount of discounted or even free admission that I compensated guests with was always justified because of the amount the guest would pay to park their car on their next visit before even stepping foot in the park. Your most successful service recovery solutions have little or no cost to the company, yield a strong value for the guest, and result in future revenue for the business.

At this point, once you have offered the most effective compensation to the guest, they have the option to accept or decline your offer. If they accept the offer, you can move immediately to the final step of thanking the guest and completing the complaint resolution successfully. If they are still not satisfied, it indicates that there is some sort of gap between the service failure and the compensation. In this case, revisit the second step in the resolution process, ensuring that the solution fits the failure directly, along with any ancillary failures that may have resulted. In many cases, the ripple effect is what gets lost in the details when a company attempts to resolve only the part that it can control.

If you have revisited the offering, presented a new solution, and the guest still does not agree, the guest will likely remain dissatisfied, and you will not be able to complete the recovery process. However, since you have made an offer, you can still follow the first rule of *always give them something*. You can close the resolution process by expressing further regret that you were unable to come to an agreeable solution, although the offer that was presented will still remain active if the guest decides to return. Keeping the offer active shows good faith on your part to rectify the solution. This strategy remains the same for guests who may refuse compensation entirely, solely for the fact that they want to be heard. As mentioned in the listening step, some people are likely to provide feedback just to make you aware of the issue, without expecting anything in return. Even though they may not accept, it shows that the compensation is being provided in return for the guest having provided the feedback, not just to recover from the complaint.

Step 4: Thank

When you have successfully resolved the guest's concern and come to an agreeable solution, the final step is following through, to wrap up the interaction neatly and put it in a figurative box that the guest will take with them to remember their experience of the resolution process, not the service failure that occurred. Similarly to the other steps, it cannot be skipped.

You have listened and understood the guest's feedback, validated their concerns, even if you may not have agreed with them, and showed that you appreciated the feedback. You expressed empathy through an effective apology that recognized the effects over the cause and assured them that their description of the events did not meet your standard. Then, the specific resolution demonstrated your desire to always give them something, ensure that the recovery fits the failure, and you have guaranteed a future visit from your guest. Even in this abridged format, you have put your guest through an emotional roller coaster that is ending on a high. And for that, the guest deserves your gratitude. Even though the recovery is essentially complete at this point, skipping this step can actually unravel the work that you have done up to this point. Thanking the guest upon completion of the recovery process holds equal weight to the three aforementioned steps.

Earlier in the process, when you expressed your appreciation for the feedback, you were thanking the guest specifically for making the complaint. While you can certainly reiterate your gratitude at this time as well, the purpose of this final step is to thank the guest for working with you directly and coming to an agreeable solution. Even if the guest was less than amenable to your help at the beginning of the process, express your pleasure for being able to resolve their issue. Then, since your recovery likely involved compensation that will be fulfilled in the future, you can thank them in advance for their future visit. There are a variety of hospitable phrases that put the icing on the cake, such as "We look forward to hosting you again in the future under better circumstances," or "We look forward to addressing these concerns directly so that you do not encounter them on your next visit." Keep it professional, but also personal and genuine. It can be easy to put together canned responses that you can either recite from a script or duplicate in writing for efficiency purposes, although guests will quickly see through that and they will lose their meaning. In order to maintain the integrity of the entire service recovery process, you must continue to *personalize the experience* by tailoring this part of the response, along with the other steps, specifically to each unique situation, and of course, using the guest's name whenever possible. Guests aren't as impressed with your copy and paste skills as they are with you having the ability to tackle difficult situations while treating guests as individuals.

What Happens after Recovery?

Because you initially segmented your guests into promoters and detractors through internal feedback collection methods, you have now used your service recovery skills to convert your dissatisfied guests, your detractors, into satisfied guests, or promoters. If done properly, you have effectively surprised and delighted them through the LAST model, and as a result, successfully executed the recovery paradox. The guest now has the likelihood of being even more satisfied than guests who were initially identified as satisfied, and they are ripe for initiating the loyalty actions, to be discussed in the next chapter. It is imperative to note that in instances of dissatisfaction, you *must* put your guests through the complaint resolution process before the items discussed in the next chapter, otherwise they will backfire, and the reverse effects may result. Instead of repeat visitation and using your guests to generate new business, you run the risk of abandonment and having your guests drive business away from you, which in essence, feeds new business to your competitors. By following the LAST model, whether it is for minor issues or larger circumstances, you demonstrate to your guests that you are both willing and able to make up for any shortcomings that they may have experienced during their visit and that you are committing to taking their experience and turning their satisfaction into loyalty.

Chapter 10 Strategy Statement:

We recognize that service failures are a natural part of the business, and we have plans in place to recover when we fail to meet our guests' expectations.

Chapter 11:
Set the Wheels in Motion

———————— 🍍 ————————

"Wow, what a lineup."

The shuttle pulled onto Canal Street, and the mood immediately turned festive. Music was coming from every direction, some of it live, some from a stereo, and the crowds were full of energy and enthusiasm. The smell was a mishmash of barbecue, confectionary, and well, maybe some other stuff too. People were having a good time. Our shuttle driver showed his permit to security to enter the French Quarter because they were significantly restricting vehicle access. He then dropped us off at our hotel, gave me his business card, and let me know that he would be happy to take us back to the airport on our way home. We all got out, grabbed our suitcases, and were ready to join the crowd and celebrate Mardi Gras.

Upon exiting the shuttle and before heading into the hotel, I looked across the street to see a massive banner on display that could be seen from a wide vantage point on Canal Street, one of the most significant arteries in the French Quarter. If I had to guess, this banner was about twenty feet wide and thirty feet tall.

Naturally, it would advertise something to do with Mardi Gras, right? See this parade from here, that parade from there, eat at this restaurant, take this tour, visit this attraction—all of these would have been applicable and even expected. But that's not what was being advertised. Instead, this colossal temporary billboard had the dates and full list of artists for the New Orleans *Jazz Festival*, taking place a couple of months later. My visit hadn't even started yet and I was already thinking about the next one, standing there and studying the lineup, thinking of which acts I would want to see. Even if I couldn't make it happen for that year's festival, the thought would still linger. I was already planning my next visit in my head.

I put the prospect of the Jazz Festival in the back of my mind, and we checked into our hotel. The next few days included a lot of live music, beignets, and king cake, and before leaving I made sure to schedule our return trip to the airport with the same shuttle driver. On the way back to the airport, the driver asked us how we enjoyed the event, and if we were planning to come back soon. Then, he made a specific suggestion. "Now that you've seen Mardi Gras, you need to come back for Halloween. It's a totally different experience, and y'all would love it."

Halloween? I'm still in Mardi Gras mode and I've got the Jazz Festival on my horizon. I guess I'll be making multiple trips back to the Big Easy . . .

Now that your guests are either satisfied with the initial experience you provided—or satisfied with your service recovery efforts—there are specific actions you can take that can influence loyalty. As stated at the beginning of this section, we cannot assume that every guest will return if satisfied, and we cannot assume that they will become ambassadors by sharing favorable word of mouth. Another fact that must be taken into consideration is that loyalty can only be influenced; it cannot be forced.

> **You cannot force your guests to be loyal, but you have many tools to help them get there.**

When determining how to set the wheels in motion for converting satisfied guests to loyal ambassadors, let's get back to the basics and recall how loyalty is defined for the purpose of this process. We know that our loyal guests do three things in particular:

1. They come back.
2. They influence others to visit.
3. They defend you.

The third action often happens organically when they are already doing the other two, so the efforts that you can put in place to encourage repeat visitation and positive word of mouth will feed into the guest defending you when necessary. Therefore, when setting the wheels in motion, you want to focus primarily on the first two actions. It is important to consider the benefits of these two actions as a result for your business if you are attempting to encourage your team toward implementing loyalty initiatives. Guest loyalty has a direct impact on the volume of business, through their own desire to return and the fact that they will be introducing new guests to you. Loyalty is not something that is "nice to have from a select few guests," but rather an achievement that every guest should qualify for, and every guest should benefit from the initiatives that you put in place.

It is also important to recognize the difference between a loyalty program and a repeat visitation incentive. Any incentive that recognizes repeat visitation can be considered one of the vehicles of getting to loyalty, but ultimately, your guests must be loyal to the product and the experience that you deliver. A promotion that suggests "Buy 10 slices and the 11th slice is free" can be effective, unless a competing pizza restaurant offers the same promotion on a similar quality product. Then what? Now it's about who makes a better pizza, and who treats their guests better.

As long as you recognize that a repeat purchase incentive is not a loyalty program, then they can be very effective as if they are loyalty training wheels. They help the guest start to take the actions that a loyal guest would, but true loyalty is when the actions continue even if the incentives and benefits are stripped away. As a reminder from chapter 2, guest loyalty is a result of the guest experience. The manner in which you exceed your guests' expectations during their visit forms the basis of the decision that guests make when determining to visit again. The Hospitality Mentality allows you to create loyalty naturally, with or without a repeat purchase incentive.

One More Competitor: Indifference

Chapter 3 covered the infinite types of competitors that you have out there, but let's add one more for fun: **indifference**. There is nothing, in particular, keeping them away from visiting again, but also nothing compelling bringing them back. Think of a time you dined out in a restaurant, said, "Wow, this was great!" and then never went back. If this sounds like you, don't feel guilty. Indifference is what happens when there was no active push to encourage your next visit or plant the seed for your next experience. In many cases, this might not have anything to do with dissatisfaction or a poor experience, and indifferent guests probably don't even know that that's how they feel. Actually, a dissatisfied experience is *preferable* to indifference because we can correct that (see chapter 10). Indifference is guest satisfaction purgatory that causes you to lose momentum when trying to turn this guest into a loyal guest. Indifference is the consequence of assuming neutral satisfaction.

Why does indifference exist? Your guest has made the effort to visit you, and you have made the distinct effort to satisfy them, and you might even feel that you're owed *something*. Anything! Tell me you loved it or hated it, just don't leave me hanging! Indifference can be incredibly frustrating because it also correlates with a lack of feedback. If your guests aren't returning because they're indifferent, you will need to refine your feedback loop (chapter 9) so you can segment a larger portion of your guests toward satisfied or dissatisfied.

Seeking feedback also helps you identify satisfied guests who may not have spoken up on their own, and it allows you to have conversations with them about areas of their experience that they enjoyed along with opportunities that there might be for improvement. If your guests are satisfied and they leave your business without being given some sort of push toward what they need to do to be loyal, you are burning energy. This is the guest experience equivalent of walking into a room, turning on the lights, and walking right out. It's like sitting in your car and slamming the gas pedal in neutral. The energy is there, but you aren't using it. Perhaps they will decide that they need to come back, but in many cases, once you're out of sight, you're out of mind, and the desire to return dwindles with every step that they take away from your facility, even if they had a positive experience. You have just done something great. Why not put forth your best effort to make it even greater? Now is the time to plant the seed for the guest's next visit, along with suggesting that they share positive word of mouth. Otherwise, you will lose more of your guests to indifference, and you deserve better.

Plant the Seed for the Next Visit

If you want your guests to come back, hopefully, they will return on their own because of the powerful experience that you provided. However, in order to increase the likelihood of repeat visitation, there are a variety of initiatives that you can implement so that you plant the seed for the next visit. The top three that I recommend are to express an invitation to return, offer a monetary incentive, and tell the guest about something they cannot experience on this visit.

1. Express an Invitation to Return

Inviting your guests to return requires no long meetings to discuss important strategic initiatives or promotions, and there is nothing more that needs to be factored into your budget. This is the overflow of your service culture that is already set to a high standard and should happen naturally when you are focused on guest interactions through the primary ways of exceeding guests' expectations discussed in part 2. This is a simple hospitable gesture that should be implemented at every level of employment and expected of any staff member who may come in contact with a guest at any time, particularly at the end of their visit, or at the end of your operating day. Telling the guest that you hope to see them again in the future costs nothing to implement, but the effects ensure a favorable lasting impression as your guest departs from their visit.

At Universal Orlando in Florida, at park closing time, team members from each attraction give a fond farewell to guests as they exit the park. This gives guests the chance to see representatives from some of their favorite attractions at the park, along with characters from their favorite movies and TV shows, as they are offered a parting salutation from a *Men in Black* agent, "Krustyland" attendants from *The Simpsons*, *Dr. Seuss* characters, Marvel superheroes, and many more. One team member is designated from each attraction daily to head from their work location to the exit of the park, where all of the attendants stand together and thank guests for visiting, inviting them to return soon. Some of them even stay in character, if possible, and they might even bring props or merchandise related to their attraction with them to continue the theming beyond the attraction themselves. It does not cost any additional labor budget, as those team members are already scheduled to be working at that time, and guests who are exiting as the park closes are treated to a hospitable departure where the staff verbally expresses their appreciation for the guests' visit along with their desire for the guest to come back in the future.

2. Offer a Monetary Incentive

Now you can put on the training wheels. As long as you recognize that presenting an incentive for the guest to return does not generate organic loyalty, you can use this to your advantage to realize the short-term goal of encouraging repeat visitation. There is no one-size-fits-all solution to this strategy, as the dynamics of each business are unique and there are significant variances from one industry to the next and each segment within each industry. However, the overall purpose of this strategy is to sweeten the pot and give the guest a financial reason to come back.

Congo River Golf, which operates several miniature golf courses throughout Florida, offers replays on rounds of golf to guests at the end of every single round. When guests finish their round and staff inquire as to how they enjoyed their game, they are then prompted with the offer to purchase another round immediately, at a substantial discount. The staff stresses that the replay does not need to be used immediately and that it has no expiration, but it is only available to purchases while they are still at the course. They also communicate that the replay is available at any Congo River Golf location, which is an effective cross-promotion strategy, as it suggests that the guest visit their other courses, as each location has a unique design. In an email conversation, Christian Vozza, Vice President of Marketing and Operations, said, "At Congo, we are all about putting smiles on our guests' faces. Encouraging them to replay or come back another time provides us the opportunity to create more fun, memorable experiences they can have with their family and friends."

Other monetary incentives to consider include coupons sent digitally to guests after their visit, discounts for joining an email list, or a loyalty program. Additionally, in theme parks and cultural attractions that offer annual passes or memberships, stressing to the guest that they can apply the value of their general admission toward the pass, along with identifying how many visits are needed to cover the cost of the pass or membership, are very successful strategies in giving the guest a monetary incentive toward coming back in the future.

3. Tell Them about Something They Cannot Do Today

You want your guests to feel both full and hungry simultaneously, either figuratively or perhaps literally. Guests are generally most satisfied when they feel that they have experienced all that there is to experience during their visit, but there are opportunities for you to suggest something that they were unable to do on this visit that keeps you on their mind as they walk out the door. Again, the best ways to implement this will vary based on your specific business, but the overall goal is to make the guest realize that even though they may have done everything there is to do on this visit (or at least nearly everything), that there will be more, different, or other experiences that they will have when they come back. If you have an extensive restaurant menu, suggest that they try a different entrée when they return. If the guest visits on a weekday but you offer enhanced entertainment on the weekends, tell your weekday guests what they can experience next time. If you have a new attraction, exhibit, or venue opening in the future, communicate this at the exit, so your guests know that they will have something else to do and see when they come back. By communicating with the guest what is going to happen next time they come, they will already begin planning their next visit, even if it is just in their mind at first.

Suggest Positive Word of Mouth

The importance of word of mouth cannot be understated. Customer experience expert Dan Gingiss knows the importance of creating a shareable experience in the interest of attracting more visitors. Dan says, "Most experiences that we have with companies are average, or boring, or so-so, or 'meh' as the millennials say, and nobody wants to share that kind of experience. Nobody has ever said, 'Let me tell you about this perfectly average restaurant I went to last night.' What they do is they either tell you, 'I went to this restaurant and it was awful and let me tell you why,' or 'I went to this restaurant and it was *amazing*, and let me tell you why.' That's what people share. My view is that if we can take all of these 'meh' interactions, all these average experiences, and turn them into something that's worth talking about, that's how we stand out from the competition because the competition has still got those average experiences."[30]

The second step in putting the training wheels in motion toward loyalty is to encourage positive word of mouth. In addition to the guest returning themselves, your loyal guests need to bring others with them. This can be both in the literal sense when their party size actually increases on their next visit, or that they have the desire to introduce new guests to your business directly. It should also be how they share the experience verbally with their personal networks, such as friends, family, and coworkers, and of course through digital platforms as well. Three of the ways I recommend extracting positive word of mouth from your guests are through offering friends and family incentives, using social media to your advantage, along with leveraging online review sites. Again, these strategies are all guest loyalty training wheels, and should all supplement the remarkable experience that you provide to your guests during their visit, rather than replace them. None of these strategies will be effective without first focusing on maximizing the guest experience and exceeding their expectations.

1. Friends and Family Incentives

Consider this step to be an extension of the *monetary incentives* strategy of planting the seed for the next visit. If you offer guests the ability to save money on their next visit, expand the offer to anyone they bring with them. In particular, this can be a highly attractive benefit to an annual pass, season pass, or membership, where the guest is already subscribing to your repeat visitation program. Since the guest is already satisfied enough that they have committed to returning, communicate that part of the value of that pass or membership is that they can bring other guests by offering them a discount on your standard offering. If you do not have a pass or a membership as part of your product lineup, you can still extend the number of guests that are eligible for the monetary incentive that you provide. If a guest sees that they can receive a 10 percent discount on their next visit for up to six people, this suggests that they should introduce new guests to your product when they return. Consider this discount to be a low cost of acquisition for generating new business through brand awareness because now we are officially talking about your guests acting on your behalf, as an extension of your marketing efforts.

2. Social Media

It would be naive of me to simply say "Be on social media" in an age where literally almost everything revolves around how people are sharing their experiences online, and have that be the substance of this message. There are countless experts, guides, and agencies that focus on increasing social media presence for businesses. In the interest of keeping it straight to the point and relevant to this part of the process in guest loyalty, I recommend considering the high-level question that pertains to social media and your business: *what are you doing to make your business more attractive on social media?* Instead of focusing only on what you are posting online through marketing initiatives, your efforts should be geared toward the content that your guests are creating. This content is organic word of mouth and carries a higher level of trust within their network of peers. Social media has already woven its way into the fabric of many of our lives and our society in general, and it should be an extension of your on-site experience. Some businesses will offer discounts for Facebook check-ins or tweets about their business or experience, and while these may be effective in the short term, focus on how you can organically foster an experience that is worthy of sharing. In addition to offering free Wi-Fi to encourage sharing, take a look at how your business supports experiences that are worthy of sharing. How appealing is your facility from a visual and photogenic standpoint?

If you went out with your friends and it didn't end up online,
did it actually happen?

Social media presents us with the twenty-first-century version of the age-old question "If a tree falls in the forest and no one is around, does it make a sound?" Case Lawrence, Founder of CircusTrix, which operates hundreds of trampoline and adventure parks internationally, knows this question well, and he takes an inside-out approach to social media. Instead of building trampoline parks, posting online, and hoping guests will share their experiences, CircusTrix designs their parks with visual stimulation in mind that naturally results in guests taking photos and videos to create shareable content. "We live in a culture that is driven by social media, and we have a population and generation that are planning their activities during the week based around social media postings."[31] The parks are designed to be highly produced photo studios. The company invests thousands of dollars at each location in painting their ceilings black because it makes selfies look better. "We are in the business of selling selfies." Case says that each of the experiences that guests can do at CircusTrix locations is a bite-size sharable moment, perfect for today's social media platforms like Instagram Stories and TikTok, where people are sharing snippets of their lives. The best social media strategy is when your guests are creating your content for you, rather than only you creating content in the hope that it gains the attention of your audience.

3. Online Review Sites

Since you initially segmented your guests into promoters and detractors to determine who was satisfied and who was dissatisfied and then intervened with your dissatisfied guests to convert them back to satisfied, now you can work toward using your satisfied guests to become your ambassadors and help bring new business to you. As stated previously, 90 percent of purchase decisions are heavily influenced by online reviews. This means that reviews are not just nice to have or don't just reinforce that you are doing a great job, but that they directly affect your inbound business. Review sites now play an integral role in today's society where they are either helping or hurting your business, and if you are doing nothing, it will gravitate toward the latter. Even if you do not fall into the vast majority of people who rely on reviews to make decisions, you cannot ignore the power of the masses who trust user-generated content more than your own marketing efforts.

You must be attentive to each of the main review sites, including Google Reviews, Facebook Reviews, Yelp, Tripadvisor, and any others where businesses like yours appear. Additionally, this is not just a responsive approach where you wait for reviews and then respond. The suggestions in chapter 10 for responding to negative reviews online are part of your online review strategy, but they're far from being the only component. You must actively recommend that your satisfied guests post online and drive them to the channel with which you most identify. There are a few methods of doing this, with the first being the hospitable approach. If you express an invitation to return, as discussed earlier in this chapter, you can tie that into your request for an online review. If your audience has your undivided attention, such as guests on a tour, in a theater, or in an office, you can explain in further detail that you rely on your most satisfied guests to spread the word by posting a review online and name your preferred channel specifically. Then, make it easy for them to get there, such as through a business card, QR code, email, or anything else that brings them to your page with minimal effort.

With so many online review sites, how do you know which is going to be the best channel for you to direct your focus? It seems excessive to ask your guests to post a review on Tripadvisor, Yelp, Facebook Reviews, and Google Reviews all at the same time. While most businesses can fall into multiple categories, especially hospitality and attractions that might have pages on all four of those platforms and more, it is important to recognize which platforms to focus on more than others. As a rule of thumb, you want to be where your audience is. If most people are using Tripadvisor to make their purchase decisions for you *and* your competitors, then that should be your area of focus. The restaurant industry has gravitated primarily toward Yelp, with less content available for other types of businesses, but that does not mean that if you don't manage a restaurant then you shouldn't consider Yelp. On Google Reviews, your ranking can help or hinder your search ranking, so it is beneficial for all businesses to be concerned with their Google ranking.

When it comes to requesting that your guests post reviews online, there is a large caveat that must be addressed. Requesting online reviews and offering return incentives are mutually exclusive initiatives, and they do not work well together. You can certainly run both strategies at the same time, but they should never be merged. It is not recommended to offer your guests any kind of incentive for posting a positive review online. I have seen businesses offer a percentage off a return visit if guests show a positive post on a review from their last visit, or some other kind of carrot dangled in front of them to influence positive feedback online. The reason why this is not recommended is that it can be considered manipulative. Even if your intentions are not ill-conceived, this can still shine an unfavorable light on you. Tripadvisor even cautions against this, indicating that reviews that are found to be incentivized will be removed, and further penalties may be applied that warn Tripadvisor readers that you may be influencing the nature of your reviews.[32]

By applying the three strategies for planting the seed for the next visit, along with the three recommended strategies for influencing word of mouth, you will successfully put the training wheels onto your guest loyalty bicycle. If you are effective in managing the guest experience and exceeding expectations, these six steps should seamlessly fall into place with your satisfied guests, and they will naturally result in greater levels of repeat visitation and positive word of mouth. As we get closer to the finish line, we now need to cover the importance of consistency in implementing all of these initiatives. Doing all of this once might show results for a brief period of time, but in order to ensure the maximum levels of success and the highest degrees of guest loyalty, everything covered up until this point should be integrated into your daily operations and be applicable to every guest, every time.

As you begin to implement these strategies and set the wheels in motion toward repeat visitation and positive word of mouth, keep in mind that it is just that: setting the wheels in motion. As we know, we cannot force our guests to be loyal, and the training wheels discussed in these chapters are to help you influence these actions to be taken. Your guests should be loyal to the experience that you provide, and none of these initiatives will be successful without first focusing on the guest experience and embracing the Hospitality Mentality. Once the training wheels are on, your most satisfied guests will be the ones who take off quicker, and the ones who are most active are the ones who most closely resemble actual loyalty. Keep a close watch on your guests who return frequently and the ones who share their experience online, particularly those who do not need the training wheels, but instead are showing their loyalty naturally. Then, work toward building momentum so that the loyalty grows organically and at a continually more rapid pace. The next chapter will talk about the conceptual framework of how guest loyalty can result in "the snowball effect" and continually build upon its own success.

Chapter 11 Strategy Statement:

We encourage our satisfied guests to return by providing compelling reasons to visit again, and we recognize that our most satisfied guests are our best marketing for influencing others to visit.

Chapter 12:
Celebrate Every Guest

et's take a brief moment and review everything that we have covered up until now. We know that guests have a high expectation when they select your business, as they should, otherwise they will select one of the other limitless options to spend their time and money. We also know that even though the expectation needs to be set considerably high, it also needs to leave room for the ability for it to be exceeded. Prior to delivering an experience that is superior to expectation, we must identify each of the specific expectations that a guest has and ensure that they can be met *before* focusing efforts on going above and beyond. Once that is complete, you can then engage your staff to make the most of every moment of truth with each guest by personalizing the experience, maintaining enthusiasm even when it may feel redundant, anticipating guests' needs by recognizing what the guest might not be able to consider on their own, and then implementing moments that "wow" guests whenever possible. Then, you will segment your guests into satisfied and dissatisfied by regularly probing for feedback and taking care of guests whose experience fell short of what they expected by using proper methods of service recovery. Then, with your satisfied guests (including guests who may not have been satisfied initially), you can use creative ways to influence repeat visitation and encourage your guests to share positive word of mouth about your business. This should then lead to them visiting again in the future, influencing others to visit as well, and defending your product when it becomes necessary. Exhale. You have just implemented nearly all of the Hospitality Mentality.

As you weave more and more of this process into your operation, your staff should feel more comfortable as they practice each component. Every guest should have the opportunity to go through this process of having their experience managed in such a well-organized manner. Then, because so much of this revolves around the guest's *next* visit, they will go through this process again when they return. You can't let your guard down, especially on a guest's return visit, because if they had a high expectation on their first visit and you exceeded it, you can bet that their expectation has been adjusted compared to what it was before.

At this point, we now know that the flow of the guest experience is not linear. It's a cycle. It's a figure eight. It's a snowball. The end of one guest's experience is the beginning of another. The influence that guests have over other prospective visitors is so powerful that they have the ability to make or break your success. You were challenged at the beginning of this book to consider the fact that every guest does not need to be visiting you and to recognize that they can do anything else. Now, I will challenge you to ask, *"How will this guest communicate their experience after they leave?"* The answer to this question lies in how well you exceed your guests' expectations and how effectively you have set the wheels in motion toward guest loyalty. Your marketing campaigns can help set the expectation for future guests, as long as you know that they are just another element in the greater mix of why people decide to visit you.

Stick with me as we add some numbers to this process and calculate the multiplicity effect that guest loyalty gives you the potential to bring. Your business is filled with many complexities. There are a lot of moving parts to the daily operation, but for the sake of this example, let us look at your business from the simplest mindset. Let's start with one guest that you would like to see become a loyal advocate. Not a couple, not a family, and not a group; this exercise is about one guest. You have calculated your average spend per guest, and for the sake of this exercise, let's say you anticipate this guest will spend a total of $30 when they visit. You put that guest through the framework of the Hospitality Mentality, ensuring to meet their expectation, and you activate all of your levers toward exceeding that one guest's expectations. You seek feedback, potentially recover from a service failure by turning it into a "wow" moment, then you sweeten the pot for their next visit and you encourage them to influence others.

That guest decides that they are going to return the following month, and the average spend per visit of $30 remains the same. Also, because of their post on Google Reviews (and from telling other people they know personally), they have influenced three other guests who otherwise had no initial intentions (or perhaps even awareness) to visit you. Instead of serving one guest, you now have four. With your structure in place, you have successfully exceeded those four guests' expectations, which includes your initial guest and three new ones, and in turn, they have also influenced three guests each. They then bring in a combined twelve additional visitors, and since they continue to return and influence, you are now at sixteen. This continues to happen every month.

On the surface, it looks like that one guest is worth $30, but we know that they are much more valuable than that. Even without influencing others, if they continue to visit once a month and spend $30 on average each visit, their value increases from $30 to $360.

1 x $30 = $30 (first visit)

12 x $30 = $360 (annually)

Since they influenced three others, we can add in the additional guests at the same average spend and include your initial loyal guest. If they all visited once, they would spend $120, yet if their loyalty also yields a monthly visit, you would gain forty-eight new visits at $30 per visit, or $1,440 in annual incremental revenue.

4 x $30 = $120 (first visits)

48 x $30 = $1,440 (annually)

In the third month, your new guests continue to influence three others, and they continue their monthly visit themselves. Each guest has a minimum value of $30 per month or $360 per year. After one year, your hospitality-focused approach to the guest experience has resulted in more than **$125 million** in additional revenue. Adjust accordingly based on your actual average spend per visitor.

If this seems like it is too good to be true, then you might be right. We are constantly facing considerable friction that is blocking us from reaching our full potential, but that shouldn't deter you from operating in this mindset anyway. What if you were successful in achieving just 1 percent of the potential results? If your service culture could generate an additional $1.25 million, would that be worth your time and energy? Then, you can work on building up to higher numbers by looking at the guest experience like a snowball. Success yields additional success. When you form a snowball, you initially pack together small clumps of snow until it is big enough that you can roll it, allowing it to pick up more snow with less and less of your guidance. When you treat that first single guest like the initial clump of snow, you guide them through the process, just like when you are putting on your training wheels in order to initiate the motion. Then, as it naturally begins to build momentum, you intervene when you need to and make sure it stays on course and continues to grow naturally.

As your snowball begins to grow, or as your loyalty momentum starts to accelerate, you always want to be mindful of the process so that you ensure that it keeps working in your favor. Because of the impacts of negative word of mouth, the loyalty snowball can also work in reverse and will usually work at a much more rapid pace. As stated in chapter 2, guests who have a negative experience may tell an average of ten *times* the number of people than guests with a positive experience. Therefore, your constant monitoring and occasional intervention in the process of guest loyalty, along with the guest experience in general, are necessary to the success of your intentions. You must **reinforce** loyalty on every visit, **engage** your staff to be on board with your mission, and **pivot** by aligning the results you desire with the results you are achieving.

Reinforce Guest Loyalty

When your community of loyal guests continues to grow, you want to take preventive measures to avoid becoming a victim of your own success. During times of high volumes of business, it can become increasingly difficult to provide a personalized experience, one of the tenets of exceeding expectations. It becomes a constant challenge to provide guests with moments that surprise and delight. Because of these growing pains that are associated with generating loyalty, you must reinforce your loyalty initiatives by building systems that make your initiatives stand out.

Naturally, the Hospitality Mentality suggests you begin with a personalized approach. By acknowledging your guests who are part of your repeat visitation program, showing appreciation for their loyalty is part of the process of removing the training wheels and taking what might appear to be manufactured loyalty and converting it into a genuine loyalty. This must also be aligned with personalizing the experience because offering a blanket statement of gratitude to a large group of people who may or may not include loyal guests does not carry the same feeling. Yes, I am referring to the canned announcement near the end of almost every flight on nearly every airline thanking all passengers, but specifically those who are frequent flier members and are earning points by spending money on that particular flight. Make it a point to regularly thank your loyal guests directly for their loyalty. The guest feels a little warmer and fuzzier when their commitment is acknowledged, and it shows that the staff sees their loyalty as genuine, not just reaping the rewards of repeat visitation.

Another way to reinforce loyalty is by offering exclusivity for your loyal guests, which your transient guests can aspire to once they break into loyalty territory. For example, hosting events that are invitation-only is a great way to engage your loyal visitors and is also an effective way to plant the seed for the next visit and to influence others. Extending an invitation to the loyal guest along with a guest of their own enables the loyal guest to introduce new business to you in a way that allows the new guest to get a small taste of what being loyal to you looks like. Alternatively, you can maintain full exclusivity and host events that only your loyal guests can attend. These types of events are perfect when they surround the opening of a new attraction or exhibit, or a preview of a seasonal event.

Lastly, build one or more "wow" moments that specifically revolve around your loyal guests. As much as you can, you want to eliminate the "been there, done that" effect if the repeatability nature of your product starts to wear off. When the front desk agent at the Ritz-Carlton offered me complimentary spa access, his reasoning was in part due to my loyalty. This instance actually happened on my third visit to that same property, but it was a new experience for me that I had not had previously. When your guests are starting to show signs of loyalty, delivering superior moments of surprise and delight will amplify their emotional attachment to your business, thus putting fuel on the fire. Consider this a turbo boost on what should already be an accelerating path toward life-long loyalty.

Engage Your Entire Organization

The strategies and initiatives discussed in this book are not just meant for leadership. They are intended to be delivered by the frontline staff, anyone with the potential of interacting with your guests, and the teams that support those departments. Therefore, elements like personalizing the experience or resolving service failures should not be an afterthought when creating your training and onboarding materials. It should be emphasized on day one of employment that among the many job duties that your frontline staff will have, exceeding expectations is as compulsory of a function as clocking in on time. Your orientation program should not just cover the mechanics of your staff members' job descriptions, but instead should focus on *why* we interact with guests in certain ways, before teaching them the nitty-gritty details of using a cash register, changing a trash can liner, or operating a roller coaster.

Conceptual guest experience training should precede on-the-job training so your staff knows what is expected from them in terms of driving loyalty through the guest experience.

If, however, you are looking to implement these processes with a team that has matured with your organization, they are likely set in their ways with how they operate and their own mentality when it comes to the guest experience. If you feel that you are falling behind where you need to be, calling it a culture shift may not resonate well with your staff, and it might generate some resentment. In this case, look to celebrate the success that you are already achieving. While I hope that there were new concepts and ideas presented in this book, I also hope that you were able to recall several specific examples of the concepts in action within your organization and your high-performing team. Take a look at how you are already incorporating many of these elements, discuss with your staff how they all lead to guest loyalty, and use it as an encouragement to continue doing it in the future. Instead of it being a culture shift, consider it to be an expansion upon the success that you are already having. When people tell me that they are already providing great service, I always respond by asking, "What's next?" In the realm of guest loyalty, there is no ceiling, and we can keep pushing to achieve the full potential of the snowball. If you feel like you have already hit the finish line, then it's time to move the goal.

Pivot as Necessary

Managing the guest experience is like tying a bow tie. When going through the steps of tying a bow tie, the finale involves gently putting one side, folded in half, through the loop that you created. Most instructions say to continually work both sides of the tie until it looks proper and mostly straight, but that there is no definitive end to the process. You can continually massage the fabric of the bow tie as much as you'd like, but it is nearly impossible for the tie to be perfectly symmetrical. The only way to have a perfect bow tie is to purchase a tie that was manufactured to be exactly straight. Therefore, having a slightly off-center bow tie that you can continue to massage demonstrates the genuine attention that went into the process.

Your process of managing the guest experience, with the ultimate goal of achieving loyalty that grows organically, is similar to the process of tying a bow tie. Once you have it in place, you must continually monitor how you are implementing each element and massage the process regularly through pivots that may be small or large. This is not a "set it and forget it" situation, where you can work on it once and then assume it is finished. Your success with maximizing loyalty is dependent on your ability to monitor the progress and locate any potential gaps in your system. In fact, the entire service recovery process is a pivot that acknowledges that you will not succeed in exceeding every guest's expectations.

However, you are still likely to encounter guest situations that are not resolved successfully, and you will still receive the occasional negative review online. *That's okay.* Besides, 78 percent of customers don't trust a perfect review rating anyway.[33] If every single one of your reviews is 5 stars (or 5 bubbles on Tripadvisor), it might mean that you aren't generating enough feedback. A 4.5 average star rating shows that you are exceptional, but also shows that you accept when honest feedback is provided. As long as your review ratings are still largely positive, they will reflect well on your prospective visitors who are conducting thorough research. Use your responses to negative reviews to win over the skeptics who might be deterred by the negative feedback. The process for responding to complaints online is also a pivot in your service recovery process because the guest has now slipped through the cracks twice. Their experience fell below the expectation, and their concerns were not able to be resolved on-site. By being aware of the instances that do not live up to your standard of excellence, you are already several steps ahead of those who implement a system that they think is foolproof. It requires constant attention and massaging, so it can regularly become closer and closer to perfection.

Your pivots should include using guest feedback to initiate change, as discussed in chapter 9. Guest complaints are an opportunity to turn the situation around for that specific guest, and they also provide you with amazing data on what you need to change, update, fix, or eliminate altogether. Regularly gaining more feedback from guests provides you with additional data that indicates what pivots you need to make. Keep in mind, this can be both positive and negative. Your most satisfied guests also provide you with data, as these are the areas that are going well that you should be continually looking to maximize. Knowing that guests are responding well to a repeat visitation incentive or another area of your loyalty training wheels shows that more resources should be allocated in that direction. Feedback is not just about finding out what you are doing wrong.

We know that there are too many barriers to allow the snowball to come to full fruition, and especially to continue growing on its own. However, you can show your guests that you are personally working toward earning their loyalty by regularly massaging your loyalty initiatives to better fit your guests' needs and measuring the success as it continues to grow. The process will never be over. You won't achieve the multiplicity effect directly of every guest coming back once a month and influencing three more who then do the same, but operating under this mentality will allow you to start to achieve it at a basic level, which you can continually refine. By reinforcing the importance of guest loyalty with your staff, along with the best ways to achieve it with every guest, you will rapidly expand upon your success, and your guests will thank you for it.

Celebrate Every Guest

It took a lot of pages to get here, but everything up to this point comes down to these three words: celebrate every guest. When you recognize that your guests don't need you and can do anything aside from visiting you, it sets the stage to celebrate every guest. When you keep your promises and meet expectations before exceeding them, you show your commitment to celebrating every guest. When you learn and use your guests' names so that you can personalize their experience, you celebrate every guest. When you maintain your enthusiasm even when answering the same question for the one hundredth time, you celebrate every guest. When you recognize that your guests don't know what they don't know and you anticipate their needs, you celebrate every guest. When you create "wow" moments that have a significant impact on their experience and their lives in general, you celebrate every guest to the extreme. When service failures occur and guests complain, you embrace the feedback and strengthen your relationship, showing that even gaps in the experience don't deter your efforts to celebrate every guest. And when you invite your guests to return and to share their feedback with others, creating loyal ambassadors out of as many guests as possible, your implementation of the Hospitality Mentality will naturally celebrate every guest.

Whether it is your slowest day of the year, your busiest, or somewhere in between, you have the ability—as well as the responsibility—to exceed the high expectations that your guests have when they visit. Celebrating every guest shows that you want to do everything you can to exceed their expectation and provide an experience so powerful that they want to come back again and tell everyone they know about your business.

Chapter 12 Strategy Statement:

We celebrate every guest.

Final Thoughts

Congratulations, you've just speared your pineapple. By inviting guests into your business and treating them as if they were in your home, they present you with an opportunity to show them that you can meet their high expectations, and even exceed them, which opens up their minds to what is possible and what can be achieved. When your guests leave, they do so with a sense of awe and wonder, and a burning desire to return. They tell others about the experience, which sparks curiosity and brings new guests directly to you.

When you recognize that your guests don't need you and they can do anything else aside from visiting you, it leads to a desire to deliver a memorable experience. The memorable experience that you deliver paves the way for lifelong loyalty. Many of the topics covered in this book, especially in part 2, focus on the creative and fun sides of service culture. Don't mistake creativity and fun for nice-to-haves, or areas of the business that don't move the needle. This *is* the business model. This *is* what moves the needle and turns normal experiences into extraordinary ones, and it builds a reputation and creates demand. In chapter 5, we even walked through how personalizing the experience can and should increase revenue. The Hospitality Mentality is a way of doing business, not an afterthought. Focus on the culture, and the money will follow.

But it's more than business. It's a way of life that brings personal satisfaction to those who deliver it, not only those who receive it. Seeing someone react when you've gone beyond their expectation should bring mutual joy, meaning at the end of each day, the sense of fulfillment that you feel is more than a transactional job well done. You're not just checking the box and moving on. This is about making a meaningful impact on people's lives that they will connect back to the business—and the individuals who made it happen.

Once, while I was speaking to a group of hospitality college students, one of the students raised their hand and asked if dealing with complaints all the time wore me down. It was a thoughtful question, and it made sense. If you regularly deal with the pressure of maintaining guest satisfaction, even in the most intense of moments, it would seem that it would drain one's energy, leading to emotional fatigue and physical exhaustion. But I thought about it for a moment, and I realized that it was actually the opposite. When given the opportunity to create a positively memorable experience—whether through a surprise and delight "wow" moment or through service recovery—the feeling at the end of the day is one of accomplishment. We may never see or hear from those guests again; therefore, we may never truly know the impact that we're making, but we do it regardless because it makes us feel good. The fact that it's good for business becomes secondary when we know that we are serving our guests to our fullest potential.

Set the expectation. Exceed the expectation. Put fuel on the fire. Create experiences that are memorable, fulfilling, and worth sharing. I hope you have enjoyed the lessons, key points, and entertaining anecdotes along the way that bring the Hospitality Mentality to life.

But we're not done! I mentioned in the introduction that there would be bonus content, and now it's time to put your plan in place. For your free implementation guide, visit **www.thehospitalitymentality.com/bonus** and get started today. This will introduce you to the philosophy, strategy, and tactics of the Hospitality Mentality, along with helping you measure your progress along the way.

As we wrap up, I have a final request. If you enjoyed this book and found it useful, please consider posting a positive review on Amazon, along with sharing what you enjoyed about the book with your network (on LinkedIn, Twitter, or your favorite social channel). Connect with me on LinkedIn if you'd like to chat further.

If this book did not live up to your expectations, I'd like to know as well. Send me a message on LinkedIn letting me know how this book could have been improved. I respond to all genuine messages.

Acknowledgments

People have asked me how long it took to write this book. While what you just read took a little over three years for me to write, the first time I started putting thoughts on paper was more than ten years before publishing, and long before I considered the title of *The Hospitality Mentality*. I have lost count of the number of times I had written a sufficient draft just to throw it out and then gain the motivation to start over again several months later. However, despite not going to print, none of those drafts were wasted; instead, I needed to wrap my head around what would truly be valuable, based on research and observations, and give concrete direction on how to apply the framework.

Fortunately, my career path since then allowed me to gain clarity on the structure of what would ultimately become this book, and I am grateful for those who have played a role in it. Thank you to Jerry Fragnito and Scott Greenwood from F&G Hospitality, Scot Carson from Amusement Advantage, and Luke Finn from ROLLER. Thank you to Matt Heller from Performance Optimist Consulting and my cohost on the *AttractionPros Podcast*—I have learned so much from getting to talk to you on Zoom at least once a week!

I'd like to thank everyone who agreed to be quoted and have their stories and lessons shared, including Simon Nash, Ruddy

Harootian, Kenny Funk, Anthony Rivera, Daine Appleberry, Joel Manby, Anthony Palermo, Andrea Bernardo, Nick Gray, Jen Rice, Christian Vozza, Dan Gingiss, and Linda Rose Hayes. Many of these stories came from podcast interviews on *AttractionPros* or *The Guest Experience Show*, which I recommend checking out. I'm also incredibly grateful for all the leadership teams who have hired me to deliver Guest Experience Workshops for their staff, along with everyone who has registered their teams for virtual workshops or webinars.

Thank you to the team at Morgan James Publishing for accepting *The Hospitality Mentality* into your amazing catalogue alongside so many other incredible authors and publications. To Catherine Turner for editing my manuscript with a fine-tooth comb, and a huge thank you to Abigail Giganan for her talented graphic design work that included the book cover, logos and branding, and additional graphics throughout the book.

To my mom, Sammi Siegel, my dad, Jon Liebman, and my stepmom, Mindy Liebman, for always encouraging me to pursue my passions and for always offering guidance along the way. And to my wife, Franny, for being my number one supporter.

About The Author

Josh Liebman specializes in guest experience within attractions, tourism, and hospitality, including service standards, complaint resolution, and driving guest loyalty. Josh is a serial entrepreneur, consultant, and speaker. Josh's educational background includes a bachelor's degree in hospitality management along with a master's degree in hospitality & tourism, both from the University of Central Florida's Rosen College of Hospitality Management.

Josh has worked for some of the top attraction operators in the world, including, but not limited to, Walt Disney World, Universal Orlando, Merlin Entertainments, and Cedar Fair. Josh has been integral to the openings of multiple venues in various leadership capacities. Additionally, Josh has consulted for many of the world's leading hospitality brands, including Ritz-Carlton, Four Seasons, Waldorf Astoria, and many more. Josh is cohost of the *AttractionPros Podcast*.

Endnotes

Chapter 1

1   Nash, Simon JC. 2022. "Creating a Culture of Hospitality (Simon JC Nash from Ohana Towels)" Interview by Josh Liebman. *The Guest Experience Show*. https://www.roller. software/the-guest-experience-show/?wchannelid=2l49v3p0c-j&wmediaid=758pf83dpk.

2   Pine, B Joseph, and James H Gilmore. 2019. *The Experience Economy: Competing for Customer Time, Attention, and Money*. Boston, Massachusetts: Harvard Business Review Press.

3   Harootian, Ruddy. 2022. "The New York Art Tour Experience (Ruddy Harootian – Ruddy Was Here)" Interview by Josh Liebman. *The Guest Experience Show*. https://www.roller. software/the-guest-experience-show/?wchannelid=2l49v3p0c-j&wmediaid=h29lypir3k.

4   "How Chick-fil-A Creates an Outstanding Customer Experience." n.d. Effective Retail Leader. Accessed August 4, 2022. https://www.effectiveretailleader.com/effective-retail-leader/how-chick-fil-a-creates-an-outstanding-customer-experience.

5   Wood, Jennifer. 2016. "10 Bizarre Hotel Guest Requests That Were Actually Granted." The Points Guy. October 8, 2016. https://thepointsguy.com/2016/10/10-bizarre-hotel-guest-requests/.

Chapter 2

6   Morgan, Blake. 2019. "50 Stats That Prove the Value of Customer Experience." *Forbes*. September 24, 2019. https://www.forbes.com/sites/blakemorgan/2019/09/24/50-stats-that-prove-the-value-of-customer-experience/?sh=22302c334ef2.

7   Thomas, Andrew. 2018. "The Secret Ratio That Proves Why Customer Reviews Are so Important." *Inc*. February 26, 2018. https://www.inc.com/andrew-thomas/the-hidden-ratio-that-could-make-or-break-your-company.html.

8   Wigginton, Dawn. 2019. "What Does a Single Negative Review Cost You?" DRAE Media & Marketing. May 12, 2019. https://draemedia.com/single-negative-review-cost/.

Chapter 3

9   Shaw, Colin. 2020. "5 Rules for Using Behavioral Science in Journey Mapping." *The Intuitive. Customer Podcast*. https://beyondphilosophy.com/5-rules-for-using-behavioral-science-in-journey-mapping/.

10 Funk, Kenny. 2021. "Episode 213 – Kenny Funk Talks about Brand Deposits, Retail as Gratuity, and One Size Fits One." Interview by Josh Liebman and Matt Heller. *AttractionPros*. http://attractionpros.com/ep213/.

Chapter 4

11 Dixon, Matthew, Karen Freeman, and Nicholas Toman. 2015. "Stop Trying to Delight Your Customers." *Harvard Business Review*. May 14, 2015. https://hbr.org/2010/07/stop-trying-to-delight-your-customers.

Part 2

12 Disney Institute Team. 2018. "Leadership Lessons from Walt Disney – How to Inspire Your Team." Disney Institute. March 21, 2018. https://www.disneyinstitute.com/blog/lead-

ership-lessons-from-walt-disney--how-to/.

Chapter 5

13 Barwick, Earl. 2017. "Awesome Experience!" Review of Audubon Zoo, New Orleans, LA. Tripadvisor. August 10, 2017. https://www.tripadvisor.com/ShowUserReviews-g60864-d10 4457-r511149158-Audubon_Zoo-New_Orleans_Louisiana. html.

Chapter 6

14 "SlotZilla Zip Line." n.d. Fremont Street Experience. Accessed August 4, 2022. https://vegasexperience.com/ fremont-zipline-slotzilla/?gclid=Cj0KCQjwyN-DBhC-DARIsAFOELTnFirBmpJAvtsSDcc4k4J0-iQQvoqtLcD-950V76F0q-aUcldQ81-CwaAgmIEALw_wcB.
15 "Beth's Burger Bar." n.d. Beth's Burger Bar. Accessed August 4, 2022. https://bethsburgerbar.com/.
16 Manby, Joel. 2020. "AP Podcast – Episode 162: Joel Manby Talks about Love, Servant Leadership and Turning a Business Around." Interview by Josh Liebman and Matt Heller. *AttractionPros*. http://attractionpros.com/ap-podcast-episode-162-joel-manby-talks-about-love-servant-leadership-and-turning-a-business-around/.

Chapter 7

17 "Omotenashi, the Japanese Philosophy That Changed Hospitality - Otolo." 2021. Myotolo.com. August 17, 2021. https://myotolo.com/omotenashi-a-japanese-philosophy-that-changed-hospitality/.
18 Anderson, Katie. 2016. "Life in Japan: Omotenashi – the Spirit of Japan's Customer Service & Hospitality." Katie Anderson. October 26, 2016. https://kbjanderson.com/life-in-japan-omotenashi-the-spirit-of-japans-customer-service-hospitality/.

19 "Dudley Do-Right's Ripsaw Falls." n.d. Universal Orlando Resort. Accessed August 4, 2022. https://www.universalorlando.com/web/en/us/things-to-do/rides-attractions/dudley-do-rights-ripsaw-falls.

Chapter 8

2 "Marriott International Announces Marriott Bonvoy – The New Brand Name of Its Loyalty Program." 2019. Marriott International News Center (US). January 16, 2019. https://news.marriott.com/news/2019/01/16/marriott-international-announces-marriott-bonvoy-the-new-brand-name-of-its-loyalty-program.

21 "Year of a Million Dreams." n.d. WDWinfo.com. Accessed August 4, 2022. https://www.wdwinfo.com/Million-Dreams.htm.

22 Hoffman, Reid. 2018. "How to Scale a Magical Experience: 4 Lessons from Airbnb's Brian Chesky." Medium. May 22, 2018. https://reid.medium.com/how-to-scale-a-magical-experience-4-lessons-from-airbnbs-brian-chesky-eca0a182f3e3.

23 Kane, Lexie. 2018. "The Peak–End Rule: How Impressions Become Memories." Nielsen Norman Group. December 30, 2018. https://www.nngroup.com/articles/peak-end-rule/#:%7E:text=Definition%3A%20The%20peak%E2%80%93end%20rule.

24 Gray, Nick. 2018. "AP Podcast – Episode 31: Nick Gray Tells Us about How His Love/Hate Relationship with Museums Resulted in a Mission to Reinvent the Experience." Interview by Josh Liebman and Matt Heller. *AttractionPros*. http://attractionpros.com/ap-podcast-episode-31-nick-gray-tells-us-about-how-his-love-hate-relationship-with-museums-resulted-in-a-mission-to-reinvent-the-experience/.

25 Rice, Jen. 2021. "Jen Rice from Whoazone." Interview by Josh Liebman. *The Guest Experience Show*. https://www.roller.software/the-guest-experience-show/?wchannelid=2l49v3p0c-j&wmediaid=arxxrsuccc.

Chapter 9

26 Willas, Smith. 2018. "7 Reasons Why Online Reviews Are Essential for Your Brand." Mention. September 26, 2018. https://mention.com/en/blog/online-reviews/.

27 "Customer Service Frustrations: Email Response Times." 2019. Arise. February 25, 2019. https://www.arise.com/resources/blog/customer-service-frustrations-series-email-response-times#:%7E:text=Over%2080%25%20of%20customers%20expect.

Chapter 10

28 Willott, Lindsay. 2019. "The Service Recovery Paradox." Customer Thermometer. November 6, 2019. https://www.customerthermometer.com/customer-retention-ideas/the-service-recovery-paradox/.

29 George, Duane. 2016. "Only 1 Out of 26 Unhappy Customers Complain. The Rest Churn." Customer Experience Magazine. April 1, 2016. https://cxm.co.uk/1-26-unhappy-customers-complain-rest-churn/.

Chapter 11

30 Gingiss, Dan. 2021. "Creating Remarkable Experiences with the WISER Method (Dan Gingiss -The Experience Maker)." Interview by Josh Liebman. *The Guest Experience Show.* https://www.roller.software/the-guest-experience-show/?wchannelid=2l49v3p0cj&wmediaid=4ixa7pxy46.

31 Lawrence, Case. 2018. "AP Podcast – Episode 21: Case Lawrence of CircusTrix Talks about Company Culture and Creating Shareable Moments in Your Business." Interview by Josh Liebman and Matt Heller. *AttractionPros.* http://attractionpros.com/ap-podcast-episode-21-case-lawrence-of-circustrix-talks-about-company-culture-and-creating-shareable-moments-in-your-business/.

32 "The Tripadvisor Incentives Policy: Why Rewarding Travel-

er Reviews Is against the Rules." 2018. Tripadvisor Insights. January 25, 2018. https://www.tripadvisor.com/TripAdvisorInsights/w591.

Chapter 12

33 Kristensen, Lars. 2018. "AP Podcast – Episode 35: Lars Kristensen of NiceJob Makes a Pretty Epic Case for Asking for More Reviews." Interview by Josh Liebman and Matt Heller. *AttractionPros.* http://attractionpros.com/ap-podcast-episode-35-lars-kristensen-of-nicejob-makes-a-pretty-epic-case-for-asking-for-more-reviews/.

A free ebook edition is available with the purchase of this book.

To claim your free ebook edition:

1. Visit MorganJamesBOGO.com
2. Sign your name CLEARLY in the space
3. Complete the form and submit a photo of the entire copyright page
4. You or your friend can download the ebook to your preferred device

A **FREE** ebook edition is available for you or a friend with the purchase of this print book.

CLEARLY SIGN YOUR NAME ABOVE

Instructions to claim your free ebook edition:
1. Visit MorganJamesBOGO.com
2. Sign your name CLEARLY in the space above
3. Complete the form and submit a photo of this entire page
4. You or your friend can download the ebook to your preferred device

Print & Digital Together Forever.

Snap a photo

Free ebook

Read anywhere

Printed in the USA
CPSIA information can be obtained
at www.ICGtesting.com
JSHW021459050224
56676JS00004B/40